INDONESIA'S

TRANSFORMATION

and the Stability of Southeast Asia

Angel Rabasa · Peter Chalk

Prepared for the United States Air Force

Approved for public release; distribution unlimited

Project AIR FORCE

RAND

The research reported here was sponsored by the United States Air Force under Contract F49642-01-C-0003. Further information may be obtained from the Strategic Planning Division, Directorate of Plans, Hq USAF.

Library of Congress Cataloging-in-Publication Data

Rabasa, Angel.
    Indonesia's transformation and the stability of Southeast Asia / Angel Rabasa, Peter Chalk.
        p. cm.
    Includes bibliographical references.
    "MR-1344."
    ISBN 0-8330-3006-X
    1. National security—Indonesia. 2. Indonesia—Strategic aspects. 3. Indonesia—Politics and government—1998– 4. Asia, Southeastern—Strategic aspects. 5. National security—Asia, Southeastern. I. Chalk, Peter. II. Title.

UA853.I5 R33 2001
959.804—dc21

                                                                    2001031904

Cover Photograph: Moslem Indonesians shout "Allahu Akbar" (God is Great) as they demonstrate in front of the National Commission of Human Rights in Jakarta, 10 January 2000. Courtesy of AGENCE FRANCE-PRESSE (AFP) PHOTO/Dimas.

RAND is a nonprofit institution that helps improve policy and decisionmaking through research and analysis. RAND® is a registered trademark. RAND's publications do not necessarily reflect the opinions or policies of its research sponsors.

Cover design by Maritta Tapanainen

Published 2001 by RAND
1700 Main Street, P.O. Box 2138, Santa Monica, CA 90407-2138
1200 South Hayes Street, Arlington, VA 22202-5050
201 North Craig Street, Suite 102, Pittsburgh, PA 15213
RAND URL: http://www.rand.org/
To order RAND documents or to obtain additional information, contact Distribution Services: Telephone: (310) 451-7002; Fax: (310) 451-6915; Email: order@rand.org

Indonesia is undergoing a systemic political transition that could lead to a variety of outcomes, from the consolidation of democracy to regression to authoritarianism or disintegration. The stakes are high. With a population of 212 million and a land mass greater than the rest of Southeast Asia combined, vast natural resources, and a strategic location straddling critical sea-lanes of communication and straits, Indonesia is the key to Southeast Asian security. Therefore, Indonesia's choices and its evolution will frame the future of Southeast Asia and influence the balance of power in the broader Asia-Pacific region.

Influencing Indonesia's transformation is the most critical challenge to U.S. foreign and defense policy in Southeast Asia. This study examines the trends and dynamics that are driving Indonesia's transformation, outlines Indonesia's possible strategic futures and analyzes their implications for regional stability and U.S. security interests, and identifies options available to the United States and the U.S. Air Force to respond to these challenges.

This research was conducted in the Strategy and Doctrine Program of Project AIR FORCE and was sponsored by the Deputy Chief of Staff for Air and Space Operations, U.S. Air Force (AF/XO), and the Commander, Pacific Air Forces (PACAF/CC). This report should be of value to the national security community and interested members of the general public, especially those concerned with U.S. relations with Indonesia and the Association of Southeast Asian Nations (ASEAN) and the future of the Asia-Pacific region. Comments are welcome and should be sent to the authors, the project leader, Dr.

Zalmay Khalilzad, or the director of the Strategy and Doctrine Program, Dr. Edward Harshberger.

PROJECT AIR FORCE

Project AIR FORCE, a division of RAND, is the United States Air Force's federally funded research and development center (FFRDC) for studies and analyses. It provides the Air Force with independent analyses of policy alternatives affecting the development, employment, combat readiness, and support of current and future aerospace forces. Research is performed in four programs: Aerospace Force Development; Manpower, Personnel, and Training; Resource Management; and Strategy and Doctrine.

CONTENTS

Preface iii

Figures vii

Tables ix

Summary xi

Acknowledgments xvii

Acronyms xix

Chapter One
   INTRODUCTION: THE REGIONAL CONTEXT 1
   Geopolitical Importance of Southeast Asia 1
   Evolution of the Southeast Asian Security Environment 3

Chapter Two
   INDONESIA'S FRAGILE DEMOCRATIC EXPERIMENT 9
   The Political Dimension: From Suharto to Wahid 9
   The Economic Dimension 15
      Economic and Social Consequences of the
         Economic Crisis 15
      The Uncertain Path to Recovery 17

Chapter Three
   THE EAST TIMOR CRISIS AND ITS CONSEQUENCES 21

Chapter Four
   THE CHALLENGE OF SEPARATISM AND ETHNIC AND
   RELIGIOUS CONFLICT 27
   Aceh: The Eye of the Storm 27

Prospects for Peace in Aceh 33
Separatism in Irian Jaya (Papua) 37
Ethnic and Religious Violence in Eastern and
       Central Indonesia 41
"Ethnic Cleansing" in Kalimantan 45

Chapter Five
REINVENTING INDONESIA: THE CHALLENGE OF
DECENTRALIZATION 47

Chapter Six
THE MILITARY IN TRANSITION 53
Organization, Missions, and Capabilities 53
The Territorial System and the Dual Function 56
Civil-Military Relations from Suharto to Wahid 59
Doctrinal Change in the TNI 63

Chapter Seven
ALTERNATIVE INDONESIAN FUTURES 67
Democratic Consolidation 67
Aborted Transition and Political Breakdown 70
Variants of Military Rule 72
Worst-Case Scenarios: Radical Islamic Rule
       and Disintegration 74
Probable Outcomes 75

Chapter Eight
REGIONAL CONSEQUENCES OF INDONESIAN
FUTURES 77

Chapter Nine
MUSLIM SEPARATIST MOVEMENTS IN THE
PHILIPPINES AND THAILAND 85
The Moro Insurgency 85
Prospects for Peace in the Philippines 92
Muslim Separatism in Southern Thailand 94

Chapter Ten
IMPLICATIONS FOR THE UNITED STATES AND THE
U.S. AIR FORCE 99

Bibliography 105

FIGURES

Map of Indonesia xx
4.1. The Moluccas (Maluku and North Maluku) 42
6.1. Major Indonesian Military Bases 55
6.2. Military Area Commands (Kodam) 57

TABLES

1.1.   Religious Composition of Central and Eastern
       Indonesia   2
7.1.   Possible Paths of Indonesian Political
       Development 68
8.1.   Regional Consequences of Indonesian
       Scenarios 79

The Republic of Indonesia, the world's fourth most populous state, is in a process of profound political transformation. Depending on how the process unfolds, Indonesia could evolve into a more stable and democratic state, revert to authoritarianism, or break up into its component parts—an Asian Yugoslavia but on an almost continental scale.

Indonesia's evolution could drive the Southeast Asian security environment in either of two directions. A successful democratic transition in Indonesia would be a factor of stability in Southeast Asia and beyond. Indonesia would become the world's largest Muslim-majority democracy—a development that could have a significant impact on the political evolution of Asia and the Muslim world. It could lead to the reconstruction of a Southeast Asian security system grounded on democratic political principles. A stable Southeast Asia would translate into reduced opportunities for potential Chinese hegemonism and, by the same token, could facilitate China's emergence as a more influential actor without destabilizing the regional balance of power.

Conversely, political deterioration or breakdown, the rise of Islamic radicalism, or, in the worst-case scenario, violent disintegration, would drive the regional security environment in the opposite direction. Southeast Asia would become more chaotic and unstable, less inviting for investment and more prone to capital flight, and more vulnerable to a bid for regional domination by a rising China.

Indonesia faces multiple interlocking challenges that threaten the survival of its fragile democratic experiment. The economy has been recovering from the depth of the 1997–1998 crisis, but the recovery remains fragile and vulnerable to exogenous and endogenous shocks. Moreover, the underlying causes of the economic crisis—the large public and private debt overhang and the insolvency of much of the corporate and banking sector—remain unresolved.

At the same time, Indonesia is facing the most serious threat to its territorial integrity since independence.[1] The separation of East Timor encouraged secessionist movements in the far more economically and politically important provinces of Aceh (in the northern tip of Sumatra), Riau, and Irian Jaya (Papua) and demands for autonomy and revenue sharing by other provinces. In tandem with secessionist threats, religious and ethnic violence has been escalating in eastern Indonesia. The growing separatist tendencies and sectarian violence are generating stresses that the Indonesian political system may not be able to withstand.

In an effort to mollify the provinces, the central government has agreed to a wide-ranging decentralization plan. This devolution of authority and resources to the provinces has a price, however. The "old" Indonesia redistributed income from the resource-rich provinces to the rest of the archipelago, especially the populous and politically dominant island of Java. The new dispensation, if implemented, could lead to the central government's loss of control over macroeconomic policy, increase the gap between the have and the have-not provinces, and create a whole new set of internal tensions that could threaten Indonesia's unity.

The military, one of the few institutions that cuts across the divisions of Indonesian society, will play a key role in the Republic's evolution. The military is withdrawing from its political role and is undergoing significant doctrinal change. It is transferring internal security functions to the newly separated national police and is considering the abandonment of its territorial command structure. Implementation of the new doctrine is far from certain and it will require enormous

---

[1]Arguably, Jakarta faced challenges that were just as serious in the Darul Islam revolt of the early 1950s, the provincial rebellions of the mid and late 1950s, and the failed Communist coup of 1965, but as Cribb and Brown point out, these were struggles over the identity of Indonesia as a whole and not over whether Indonesia would survive in its existing configuration. Robert Cribb and Colin Brown, *Modern Indonesia: A History Since 1945*, Longman, London and New York, 1995, p. 160.

changes in the military's organizational structure, training, and personnel practices.

Indonesia's prospects for the short to medium term (one to three years) are for a continuation of weak governments and worsening of security conditions in provinces experiencing separatist or communal violence. President Wahid may resign or be removed from office if he fails to reverse the erosion of his political support, but a successor government, presumably headed by current Vice President Megawati Sukarnoputri, would not necessarily produce greater stability. Over the longer term, barring a lasting upturn in the economy or a workable agreement with disaffected provinces, the odds are better than even that one or more of the downside scenarios described in Chapter Seven—a variant of military rule, an Islamic-dominated government, or national disintegration—could come to pass.

The overriding challenge for the United States is how to help shape Indonesia's evolution so that it will emerge as a stable democracy and as a capable partner in maintaining regional security and stability. The ability of the United States to engage the Indonesian government and military will be shaped by two factors: the domestic environment in Indonesia and the geopolitical environment in Asia. Indonesia's evolution as a stable democracy would make it easier for the United States to forge closer ties, particularly in the military sphere. On the other hand, if the geopolitical environment in Asia became more threatening, the need to work with the Jakarta government to restore security and stability in the region could override other U.S. policy interests in Indonesia.

How should the United States reconcile its priorities with regard to Indonesia? A possible approach is to establish a baseline for U.S. engagement with Indonesia—defined in terms of what the United States should do now. The level of engagement could be increased or decreased depending on changes in conditions in Indonesia, Southeast Asia, and the broader Asia-Pacific region. Steps that the United States could immediately take include:

- Support for Indonesia's stability and territorial integrity, both for strategic reasons and because a stable and secure Indonesia is also more likely to be democratic. First, the United States should work with Japan, other regional allies, and the international financial institutions to provide the resources needed to assist Indonesia in overcoming its multiple crises. Second, support for Indonesia's democratization and stability should not be made contingent on the resolution of second-tier issues. Third, the United States and the international community should refrain from demanding more than the weakened Indonesian government can deliver, particularly on issues that touch on sensitive sovereignty concerns. In this regard, it is important to be cognizant of how giving or withholding aid for Indonesia plays in Indonesian politics—a miscue could result in weakening rather than strengthening Indonesian democratic forces. It is also important to set the correct *tone* of the public dialogue with Indonesia. Indonesian political culture places great value in indirection and ambiguity, and a perceived confrontational or condescending approach would likely prove to be counter-productive.

- Closer military-to-military ties. The United States has an oppor-tunity to influence the thinking and evolution of the Indonesian military at a time when that institution is looking for a new model and is open to new ideas. To shift from a territorial-based force with an internal security mission to a modern military focused on external defense, the Indonesian armed forces need the technical support and training that the U.S. military can provide. At the same time, deeper engagement with the Indonesian military would improve the ability of the United States to promote a democratic model of military pro-fessionalism. It would also enable the United States to involve Indonesia as a full partner in efforts to foster intra-ASEAN defense cooperation and interoperability.

- Assistance to prevent the further deterioration of Indonesian defense capabilities, particularly air transport. An Indonesia that lacks the capability to defend itself or respond to outbreaks of ethnic or religious violence would be less likely to achieve a successful transition to a stable democracy and could become a source of regional instability. The escalating sectarian violence in eastern Indonesia makes the rapid deployment of troops to trouble spots a critical need. Restoring Indonesia's air transport capability should be a priority of U.S. assistance.

- Helping to restore Indonesia's regional security role. This would be necessarily a long-term goal, because Indonesia is unlikely to resume its leadership role in Southeast Asia until the country overcomes its current domestic difficulties. The United States could move the process forward by helping to restore, to the extent possible, the Indonesian-Australian security relationship, which was in the past an important element of the Southeast Asian security architecture. The Australian-Indonesian relationship took a turn for the worse as the result of the East Timor crisis. Restoring it will not be easy. Nevertheless, the United States, as a treaty ally of Australia and friend of Indonesia, can help facilitate a necessary rapprochement between these two key regional actors.

- Designing a permanent solution to the East Timor question. A key part of the rebuilding of a constructive Indonesian role in regional security is securing a stable, independent East Timor and a constructive relationship between Indonesia and East Timor. Attaining this goal will require a two pronged-strategy: (1) promoting the negotiation of an arrangement that takes into account the interests of all sides and (2) organizing an international effort to train and equip an East Timorese security force capable of securing the border and protecting the East Timorese population from recalcitrant militia factions. Such a settlement would make possible the return of refugees and the closing of the camps in West Timor and should include the cessation of Indonesian support for the militia elements.

At the same time, the United States and the U.S. Air Force need to plan for contingencies that could arise if the situation in Indonesia were to deteriorate further. Such contingencies could include, for instance, a noncombatant evacuation of U.S. and third-country nationals, a major humanitarian crisis, or the escalation of conflict in Timor. Enhancing the United States' ability to respond to these and other contingencies would require deepening the web of defense relationships with and among friendly regional states, particularly those with whom the United States enjoys treaty or close defense relationships, such as Australia, the Philippines, and Singapore.

Over the longer term, if Indonesia were to overcome its current domestic problems, the United States and Indonesia could further

xvi   Indonesia's Transformation and the Stability of Southeast Asia

develop a cooperative defense relationship. This relationship may include access arrangements as a part of the diversification of U.S. access and basing arrangements in the Asia-Pacific region discussed in other RAND work.[2]

---

[2]See Zalmay Khalilzad et al., *The United States and Asia: Toward a New U.S. Strategy and Force Posture*, RAND, MR-1315-AF, 2001; Richard Sokolsky, Angel Rabasa, and C. R. Neu, *The Role of Southeast Asia in U.S. Strategy Toward China*, RAND, MR-1170-AF, 2000.

ACKNOWLEDGMENTS

The authors wish to thank all those who made this study possible. Our most important sources were government and military officials, academics, and research institutions in Indonesia, Singapore, the Philippines, and Thailand. We thank the director and staff of the National Resilience Institute (LEMHANNAS) of Indonesia, the Centre for Strategic and International Studies of Indonesia, the National Defense College of the Philippines, and the Institute of Defence and Strategic Studies (IDSS) of Singapore. For important insights on the Indonesian economy, politics, and military affairs, we are indebted to Dr. Indria Samego, Brigadier General TNI (ret.) Soedibyo, Dr. Hadi Soesastro; and Lieutenant Generals TNI Johny Lumintang and Agus Widjojo, whom we had the pleasure of hosting at the RAND Washington office in March 2000. For the Washington-based analyst, the series of conferences organized by the United States-Indonesia Society (USINDO) have been an invaluable resource. We also benefited from events organized by the Johns Hopkins University Paul H. Nitze School of Advanced International Studies (SAIS) and the Conference on Security Cooperation in the Asia Pacific (CSCAP).

We further thank the reviewers of this report, Dr. James Clad of Georgetown University, and Colonel John Haseman, USA (ret.), former U.S. defense attaché in Jakarta, for many useful insights. Within RAND, we thank Zalmay Khalilzad, Corporate Chair in International Security. Dr. Khalilzad supervised a series of studies on Asian security issues that provided the intellectual framework for this project. We also thank Edward Harshberger, director of the Strategy and Doctrine Program, Project AIR FORCE, and C. R. Neu for their review of the manuscript. Not least, we thank our editors, Jeanne Heller and Phillip Wirtz, our production editor, Christopher Kelly, and our assistant, Joanna Alberdeston.

ABRI	Angkatan Bersenjata Republik Indonesia (Armed Forces of the Republic of Indonesia)
Bulog	State Logistics Agency
GAM	Gerakan Aceh Merdeka (Free Aceh Movement)
INTERFET	International Force on East Timor
Kodam	Komando Daerah Militer (Military Area Command)
Korem	Komando Resor Militer (Military Resor Command)[1]
Kodim	Komando Distrik Militer (Military District Command)
Koramil	Komando Rayon Militer (Military Subdistrict Command)
MPR	Majelis Permusyawaratan Rakyat (People's Consultative Assembly)
OPM	Organisasi Papua Merdeka (Free Papua Organization)
TNI	Tentara Nasional Indonesia (Indonesian National Military)

---

[1]There is no satisfactory English translation of the Indonesian military term "resor."

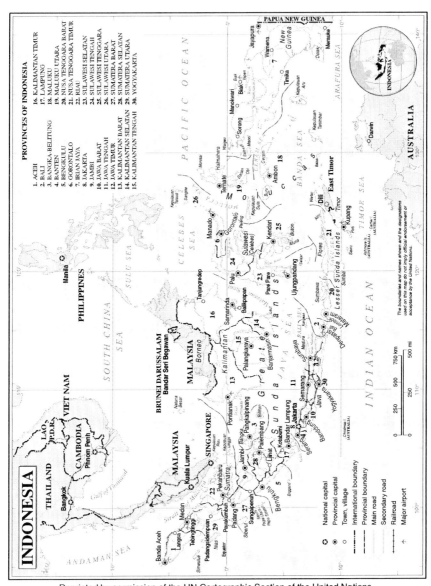

INDONESIA

Chapter One

INTRODUCTION: THE REGIONAL CONTEXT

GEOPOLITICAL IMPORTANCE OF SOUTHEAST ASIA

Southeast Asia derives its geopolitical importance from the region's location at the crossroads between the concentration of industrial, technological, and military power in Northeast Asia, the Indian sub-continent and the oil resources of the Middle East, and Australia and the Southwest Pacific. A high proportion of the trade of Japan, the Republic of Korea, Taiwan, and Australia, including much of their oil imports, transits the straits and sea-lanes of communication in Southeast Asia.[1] From a military perspective, these sea-lanes are critical to the movement of U.S. forces from the Western Pacific to the Indian Ocean and the Persian Gulf.

Southeast Asia is also important as the cultural as well as the geographic crossroads of Asia, where Sinic, Hindu, Islamic, and Western civilizations have met and interacted for almost a millennium.[2] If national boundaries were replaced with ethno-religious boundaries, one would find a far-from-homogeneous Muslim arc from southern

---

[1]Shipping transiting the region must pass through one of three or four chokepoints: the straits of Malacca, Sunda, or Lombok, or possibly the straits east of East Timor. See John H. Noer, *Chokepoints: Maritime Economic Concerns in Southeast Asia*, National Defense University, Washington, D.C., 1996.

[2]Trade routes linking peninsular and insular Southeast Asia to China and India began to emerge in the first century A.D. Islam had become entrenched in the Malayan peninsula and Sumatra by the thirteenth century and spread widely in Southeast Asia from the fourteenth to the seventeenth centuries. European colonization began with the Portuguese capture of Malacca, center of the most important Malay state, in 1511, and the Spanish settlement of Manila in 1571.

Thailand, through the Malaya peninsula, Sumatra, Java, the coastal areas of Borneo, to the Sulu archipelago and parts of Mindanao in the southern Philippines; strong Christian, animist, or mixed communities in the Moluccas, Sulawesi, Kalimantan (Borneo), Nusa Tenggara, and Irian Jaya (Papua); a Hindu majority in Bali; a predominantly Catholic population in the Philippines; diverse cultures, largely Buddhist, in mainland Southeast Asia; and Chinese communities spread throughout the region. Muslims constitute almost 90 percent of Indonesia's population, but as shown in Table 1.1, Christians and other non-Muslims constitute majorities or principal minorities in several provinces in eastern and central Indonesia.

With the weakening of government structures as the consequence of the economic crisis, the ethno-religious divides in a number of Southeast Asian countries have taken on greater salience. The struggles that play out in the region, therefore, may have an influence well beyond the Southeast Asian area. How Indonesia, the world's largest Muslim majority country, deals with the issues of democracy and

Table 1.1

Religious Composition of Central and Eastern Indonesia (percent)

Province	Muslim	Christian	Other
East Kalimantan	85.68	13.55	0.77
Central Kalimantan	69.91	18.39	11.70
West Kalimantan	56.34	30.18	13.48
South Kalimantan	96.75	1.37	1.88
North Sulawesi	44.10	52.00	3.90
Central Sulawesi	76.23	19.42	4.35
South Sulawesi	88.50	9.70	1.80
Southeast Sulawesi	96.27	2.42	1.31
West Nusa Tenggara	95.90	1.00	3.10
East Nusa Tenggara	9.12	86.05	4.83
Maluku	56.79	42.70	0.51
Irian Jaya	15.00	83.00	2.00

SOURCES: Indonesian Provinces of EAGA (East ASEAN Growth Area) in http://www.brunet.bn/org/bimpeabc/Idprov.htm and The Indonesian Provinces in www.indonesia-ottawa.org/indonesia/provinces.

political and religious diversity, for instance, could resonate in Asia and the broader Islamic world. A successful democratic experiment in Indonesia would go a long way in discrediting the claim that democracy may not be compatible with the political culture of Muslim countries.

Moreover, with a population of over 500 million, a wealth of natural resources, and economies growing at rapid rates before the 1997–1998 economic crisis, Southeast Asia is a significant component of the Asian and global balance of power. From the standpoint of U.S. economic security, the region's importance increased exponentially over the past decade as the region became more integrated into the global economy. Indeed, Southeast Asia was second only to Japan and well ahead of China and Hong Kong in terms of U.S. exports to the Pacific Rim in the 1993–1997 period.[3] Although U.S. exports to the region fell by some 20 percent in the immediate aftermath of the Asian financial crisis, robust trade growth is expected to resume when the region reemerges from the crisis. It should also be pointed out that Southeast Asia has been a major destination of U.S. direct investment, surpassing Japan and Brazil by 1997.[4]

EVOLUTION OF THE SOUTHEAST ASIAN SECURITY ENVIRONMENT

Over the last three decades, Southeast Asia evolved as a loose security community under Indonesian leadership. The geopolitical events that made possible the evolution of Southeast Asia as a security community were the failed 1965 Communist-backed coup in Indonesia, the fall of Sukarno, and the establishment of the New Order regime under Suharto. The Republic's new leader quickly moved to end the confrontation (*"konfrontasi"*) with Malaysia and aligned Indonesia politically with the conservative governments of the states that were to become the Association of Southeast Asian Nations (ASEAN).[5]

---

[3]*U.S. Statistical Abstract 1998*, No. 1323, p. 801.

[4]*Survey of Current Business*, July 1998, Table 3.2.

[5]The original members were Indonesia, Malaysia, Singapore, Brunei, the Philippines, and Thailand.

The key predicates upon which this regional community rested were that political stability, in most cases in the context of authoritarian political structures, social harmony (the so-called Asian values), and economic modernization constituted a paradigm of development more suitable to Asian conditions than Western models. The ASEAN Way, as it came to be known, also emphasized multilateral cooperation—primarily but not exclusively through informal ASEAN mechanisms—as the preferred path to resolution of regional conflicts and disputes; decisionmaking through consensus; and nonintervention in each other's internal affairs.

Until the second half of the 1990s, the ASEAN model constituted what appeared to be one of the world's most successful examples of regional cooperation. The havoc wreaked by the economic crisis of 1997–1998, however, undermined important conditions of the old model.[6] At the same time, ASEAN's decision to expand its membership by incorporating Vietnam, Laos, Cambodia, and Burma (Myanmar)—far less developed states, with rudimentary market economies and more authoritarian and in some cases neo-Communist political cultures—diluted ASEAN's cohesion and further paralyzed its decisionmaking process.[7]

ASEAN's diplomatic coherence and convergent purpose were severely weakened by the economic crisis and associated political upheavals in some of its principal members, notably Indonesia. With Indonesia beset by grave domestic problems and with its very future uncertain, Jakarta has been unable to exercise its customary regional leadership. ASEAN therefore has been left to drift, as was demonstrated by its passive role during the East Timor crisis of 1999, even though several member countries participated in the peacekeeping International Force for East Timor (INTERFET) and the United Nations Transitional Administration in East Timor.

---

[6]The Asian economic crisis began as financial and currency crises and then developed into massive recessions that affected the real economies of Thailand, Indonesia, Malaysia, the Philippines, and Korea. The consequences for Indonesia are described in Chapter Two.

[7]See James Clad, "Fin de Siecle, Fin de l'ASEAN?" Pacific Forum Center for Strategic and International Studies (CSIS), PacNet Newsletter.

Second, the so-called Asian model of development has become less tenable, at least in the more economically and politically developed countries of the region.[8] The demise of this model has been most apparent in Indonesia, but there are also widening cracks in Malaysia, where Prime Minister Mahathir sought to maintain the status quo through economic policies designed to insulate Malaysia from global capital markets and by heavy-handed repression of political opponents.

Third, there has been a weakening of the non-intervention doctrine. Philippine Foreign Minister Siazon's meeting with Burmese dissident Aung San Suu Kyi during then President Ramos' visit to Burma (Myanmar) in 1998 represented an early crack in the model. The public criticism in the Singaporean press of the Indonesian government's failure to prevent or control the fires in Sumatra and the resulting "haze" in 1997–1998 was unprecedented. Former Philippine President Estrada's protest of Mahathir's treatment of his former Deputy Prime Minister, Anwar Ibrahim, and the Thai proposal to replace non-intervention with a new concept of "constructive criticism" (since renamed "flexible engagement") are indicative of this change.

Fourth, there has been an increase in ethnic and religious conflict and the growth of separatist movements. The collapse of the Suharto order led to the separation of East Timor and a loss of central authority over many provinces, emboldened armed separatist movements in Aceh and Irian Jaya (Papua), and unleashed large-scale ethnic and religious violence in the Moluccas, Sulawesi, and Nusa Tenggara. In the Philippines, both Communist and Islamic insurgencies have intensified. Armed Islamic separatist activity continues in southern Thailand. Malaysia has escaped a resumption of conflictive ethnic politics, but the growth of Islamic fundamentalism

---

[8]The Asian model of development is a contested phrase in political economy. For purposes of this analysis, the key predicates of the model, as applied in Southeast Asia, are defined as follows: (1) political stability, in some cases in the context of authoritarian political structures; social harmony; and state-guided economic growth and modernization as a model of development more suitable to Asian countries than Western democratic free-market models; (2) multilateral cooperation, primarily but not exclusively through informal ASEAN mechanisms, as the preferred path to resolution of regional conflicts and disputes; and (3) noninterference in the internal affairs of other states.

and the political gains registered by the Islamic Party of Malaysia (PAS) in recent years are potential factors of instability.

Fifth, and paralleling this development, there has been a broadening of the ASEAN security agenda, which now includes challenges as diverse as piracy, drug trafficking, and illegal migration. The 1997 economic meltdown played a key role in promoting the salience of these threats, with more and more people resorting to black market activities as a way of "compensating" for falling wages, higher prices, and job losses.

Illegal migration is increasingly viewed as a security problem. There are hundreds of thousands of illegal Indonesian migrants in Malaysia, including many Acehnese suspected of links with secessionist organizations in Indonesia. In April 1998, in an effort to avoid deportation, several dozen Indonesians forced their way into a number of embassies and the United Nations mission in Kuala Lumpur. The operation was apparently orchestrated by the Acehnese separatist organization, *Gerakan Aceh Merdeka* (GAM), or Free Aceh Movement. Narcotics trafficking has long been endemic, particularly in mainland Southeast Asia, but it has taken on new dimensions— including traffic in metamphetamines, which the Thais consider a major security concern.

One particularly troubling phenomenon that has emerged in this regard is an increase in piracy, which now involves a wide spectrum of attacks ranging from opportunistic robberies against ships at port to the outright hijacking of oceangoing vessels and cargo containers.[9] Assaults have been especially rife in the seas off Indonesia. Increased motivation for engaging in maritime crime, combined with declining resources for coastal surveillance, has been reflected in a growing zone of lawlessness around the archipelago, with no fewer than 277 attacks taking place in the 1997–1999 period. This represented over one third of all attacks recorded around the world during the three

---

[9]See Peter Chalk, "Contemporary Maritime Piracy in Southeast Asia," *Studies in Conflict and Terrorism*, Vol. 21, No. 1, 1998.

years and 76 percent of the incidents reported in Southeast Asia during this period.[10]

Finally, there has been a major fraying of the Indonesian-Australian security relationship. Although not a direct consequence of the economic crisis, Indonesian-Australian security cooperation suffered serious damage as the result of the East Timor crisis and a change of policy priorities in Canberra.[11] Australia was one of only two countries that recognized the Indonesian annexation of East Timor in 1975. The East Timor crisis challenged the premise of Australia's policy of engagement with Indonesia at the time when the Keating Liberal party government, associated with a policy of rapprochement with Jakarta, was replaced by the Howard-led Labor party government. Australian public opinion turned against the Keating policy of engagement after the violent backlash of pro-Indonesian militias on East Timor in September 1999. This provided the political context for Canberra's decision to intervene in the province as the head of INTERFET. The perceived humiliation enraged Indonesian nationalists and fueled anti-Australian and anti-Western sentiment. Bilateral relations have since progressively deteriorated and are at their lowest point in 30 years. Indicative of this trend was Jakarta's cancellation of the Australian-Indonesian Mutual Agreement on Security, which had been signed in 1995.[12]

The near-term strategic implication of these changes in the regional security environment is a diminished ability of the ASEAN states to counter security threats. The unstable regional security environment presents unprecedented opportunities for internal and external

---

[10]Regional Piracy Centre, *Piracy and Armed Robbery Against Ships,* ICC-International Maritime Bureau, London, January 2000, p. 3. See also Peter Chalk, "Maritime Piracy: A Global Overview," *Jane's Intelligence Review,* Vol. 12, No. 8, 2000, pp. 47–50.

[11]For a discussion of Australia's Indonesian policy under successive Australian governments and the role of East Timor in Australia's policy, see James Cotton (ed.), *East Timor and Australia,* Australian Defence Studies Centre, Canberra, 1999.

[12]The Australian intervention in East Timor has been described as a tactical success but a strategic failure—because it signaled the failure of Australia's efforts to create multilateral security institutions to deal precisely with crises of this nature and because Australia was perceived by Asians as behaving as an arrogant "European" power. Thomas-Durell Young, "Australian Security and Defense Posture: Implications for Effecting Greater Cooperation," discussion paper, Pentagon Study Group on Japan and Northeast Asia, July 24, 2000.

actors—whether political dissidents, religious extremists, separatists, or prospective hegemons—seeking to overturn the status quo or achieve regional dominance.

In the medium to long term, the shape of the regional security environment will depend on the ability of decisionmakers in the most at-risk countries, particularly Indonesia and the Philippines, to counter threats to political stability and national cohesion, promote economic recovery, and develop stronger structures of security cooperation.

Chapter Two

INDONESIA'S FRAGILE DEMOCRATIC EXPERIMENT

THE POLITICAL DIMENSION: FROM SUHARTO TO WAHID

The regional economic crisis aside, the political crisis in Indonesia that brought down Suharto's New Order regime was the major geopolitical event in Southeast Asia in the past 30 years, comparable in some ways to the events of 1965. The eclipse of Sukarno and the abandonment of Sukarno's confrontational policy toward Malaysia and the Western powers in the aftermath of the 1965 coup made possible the creation of the new Southeast Asian order. Suharto's resignation in May 1998 pointed to the unraveling of that order. Suharto's fall released a new set of political forces and diminished the power of the institutions that underpinned his regime.[1]

Beyond that, there has been a perceptible change in Indonesia's political culture. The authoritarian bureaucratic-military vision of the state and society that dominated in the Suharto era has been replaced by a greater emphasis on civil society and political parties as the primary focus of order and stability. The parliament is now more powerful and legitimate than at any time since the 1950s. The presi-

---

[1]A different view, offered by Professor James Clad in his review of this report, is that Suharto's fall increased rather than diminished the power of some of these institutions—for example, the military and the state corporations—that were tightly controlled by Suharto during his rule. See also Damien Kingsbury, "The Reform of the Indonesian Armed Forces," *Contemporary Southeast Asia,* Vol. 22, No. 2, August 2000, p. 304. While the power of such institutions vis-à-vis the presidency may be greater than under Suharto, their power (and that of the centralized state as a whole) has decreased in absolute terms and vis-à-vis civil society and emerging regional power centers.

dent was limited to two five-year terms and was made answerable to the legislature once a year. The media, tightly controlled under the New Order, is one of the freest in Asia.

Despite the magnitude of the changes, the constitutional forms were maintained as power passed from Suharto to his vice president, B. J. Habibie, and from Habibie to Abdurrahman Wahid. Habibie turned out to be a transitional figure. A technocrat who owed his position entirely to his personal relationship with Suharto, Habibie lacked a power base in either the military or the ruling political party, Golkar, and found his legitimacy questioned by the opposition forces. Under these conditions, Habibie felt obliged to call for new parliamentary elections and the convening of the People's Consultative Assembly (*Majelis Permusyawaratan Rakyat* or MPR), the body charged with electing the president, to secure a fresh mandate. This was not an entirely unreasonable expectation. Habibie could count on the nationwide Golkar organization, the considerable power and resources available to the president, and the possibility of manipulating the cumbersome electoral process to secure his political objective. The risk was reopening the presidential selection process.

The June 1999 election of the *Dewan Perwakilan Rakyat* (DPR), Indonesia's parliament, was an "emergency election." The last parliamentary election was held in 1997, and the next one was not scheduled until 2002. At stake were 462 seats in the 500-member DPR (38 seats were reserved for the military). The president was to be chosen by the MPR, which includes the 500 members of parliament and 200 additional members, of which 135 were chosen by provincial legislatures and 65 were selected to represent social groups and organizations.

The election was a watershed event—the first genuinely free election in Indonesia since Sukarno's introduction of "Guided Democracy" in the late 1950s. Of the 48 parties that contested the election, five emerged as major players:

1. Megawati Sukarnoputri's Indonesian Democratic Party–Struggle (PDI–P), with 35 percent of the vote. The PDI-P represents the legacy of Megawati's father, Indonesia's founding President Sukarno, and the political forces he represented. The PDI–P base of support encompassed the old Sukarnoist strongholds in cen-

tral and east Java, as well as Christian and Hindu communities. Although herself a Muslim, Megawati was criticized by the overtly Muslim parties for the relatively large number of Christians in the PDI–P lists for the parliamentary election.

2. Golkar, the former government party, with 22 percent. Golkar's support collapsed in Java, but the party retained its political machinery and strength in areas outside Java. (Golkar did well outside of Java not only because its machinery remained intact but because Habibie, the party's titular leader, was *not* from Java— with Wahid's selection the presidency returned to Javanese hands.)

3. Abdurrahman Wahid's National Awakening Party (PKB), 12 percent. The PKB is the political arm of the traditionalist Nahdlatul Ulama, the Muslim world's largest mutual help organization, founded by Wahid's father and led by Wahid.

4. The Islamic United Development Party (PPP), 11 percent. The PPP was established as a religious party under the New Order through a consolidation of a number of small Islamic parties. It competed for the Islamic vote with smaller militant Islamic parties as well as the PKB and the Islamic National Mandate Party.

5. The Islamic National Mandate Party (PAN), 8 percent. Led by Amien Rais, a University of Chicago-educated former leader of the modernist Islamic mutual aid organization Muhammadiyah (the second largest mass movement in Indonesia, after Wahid's Nahdlatul Ulama).

Religion was not a central issue in the election. Although both Wahid's PKB and Rais' PAN tapped into Islamic communities and organizations for support, their leaders stressed tolerance and pluralism. Militant Islamic parties received less than 6 percent of the vote.[2] Dr. William Liddle saw in the election the rise of the society against the state. The state bureaucracy and the military, which had been used by the Suharto regime to ensure government victories since

---

[2]See the analyses by Sabam Siagian, Taufik Abdullah, and William Liddle in United States-Indonesia Society (USINDO), "Parliamentary Elections in Indonesia: Consensus, Coalitions, or Confusion?" *Proceedings of USINDO Workshop*, Washington, D.C., June 22, 1999, pp. 10–16.

1970, did not appear to have played a major role in the 1999 election in Java, although Golkar's residual influence in the outer islands helped it to secure a better-than-expected share of the vote.[3]

Meeting in October 1999, the People's Consultative Assembly (MPR) unexpectedly elected Abdurrahman Wahid, better known as Gus Dur, as the new president. The vote for Wahid, who was on record as supporting Megawati's candidacy, was the result of a move by Golkar and the Islamic parties to block Megawati's election. Tensions were defused when Wahid offered Megawati the vice presidency and she accepted.

At first glance Wahid, a nearly blind cleric in frail health, known for his idiosyncratic behavior, appeared to be an unlikely candidate for the presidency.[4] In fact, despite his shortcomings, Wahid probably represented the best compromise that could be achieved; he may have been better poised to promote national conciliation and cohesion than any of the alternatives. As former Ambassador to Indonesia Paul Wolfowitz pointed out, after Wahid's ascension to the presidency he lived up to his reputation for being inclusive and protective of the rights and safety of religious and ethnic minorities.[5]

Wahid's election as president marked a critical milestone in the transition from the New Order to a more democratic political system. As an Indonesia expert noted, in its later stage Suharto's rule had come to resemble the imperial Dutch governor-generalship,

---

[3]Ibid., p. 14.

[4]James Clad notes that Wahid's erratic behavior comes from survival strategies in Suharto-era Indonesia that still serve him well, up to a point. Personal communication, November 2000.

[5]Paul Wolfowitz, "A Muslim leader with a difference," *Wall Street Journal*, November 11, 1999. For the sources of Gus Dur's political thinking, see Mark R. Woodward (ed.), *Toward a New Paradigm: Recent Developments in Indonesian Islamic Thought*, Arizona State University Press, Tucson, 1996. Woodward emphasizes the Islamic tradition of consensus and analogy and ninth century Sufi mysticism, which informs the way in which millions of Muslims in Java think about moral and ethical problems. According to Woodward, Gus Dur does not believe that Islamic law mandates a specific political system and that democracy provides the best way to fulfill the social teachings of the Koran. Presentation at United States-Indonesia Society (USINDO) Conference, Washington, D.C., November 30, 1999.

supplemented with resonances of precolonial divine kingship.[6] Although the 1945 constitution gives the president great powers, there has been in effect a dispersal of power from the presidency to other institutions. The parliament is now more powerful and legitimate. The structure of social control constructed during the New Order is being dismantled. In March 2000, Wahid ordered the dissolution of the Agency for the Coordination of Support for National Stability Development (Bakorstanas), an organization headed by the armed forces commander charged with identifying potential threats to national security and viewed as a tool of repression by many Indonesians. Also abolished was the *litsus* system, an examination of the political background of civil servants.[7]

Nevertheless, several factors make the transition to a stable democracy a difficult and unpredictable process. Wahid's erratic style of governance, strains between Wahid and Vice President Megawati Sukarnoputri and their adherents, and the erosion of the coalition that brought Wahid to power are some of these factors. Lack of agreement within the governing coalition on problems such as the privatization of state-owned enterprises, the process of decentralization, and economic and fiscal policy resulted in protracted controversies within the Wahid administration.[8] The reputation of the Wahid government was also damaged by a series of scandals, most notably the disappearance of funds donated by the Sultan of Brunei for Aceh relief work and the illegal transfer of some Rp 35 billion (US$4.2 million) from the State Logistics Agency (Bulog) to the president's former masseur, who claimed to be acting in the president's name. One of Indonesia's political commentators described the Wahid government "as corrupt as the Suharto era," but less efficient.[9]

Wahid's deteriorating relationship with the parliament was highlighted by the controversy over his dismissal of two cabinet ministers

---

[6]Michael van Langenberg, "End of the Jakartan empire?" *Inside Indonesia*, No. 61, January-March 2000.

[7]International Republic Institute, *Weekly Update*, March 10, 2000.

[8]Presentation by Faisal Basri, Indonesian economist and political leader, U.S.-Indonesian Society (USINDO), Washington, D.C., July 21, 2000.

[9]Presentation by Dr. Sjahir, United States-Indonesia Society (USINDO), Open Forum, Washington, D.C., January 3, 2001.

in April 2000—Minister of Investment and State-Owned Enterprises Laksamana Sukardi, a confidant of Vice President Megawati Sukarnoputri, and Jusuf Kalla—on charges of graft. Wahid, however, was unable to produce any evidence of these allegations and in July, 200 members of the MPR signed a petition demanding an explanation of the ministers' dismissal.[10]

As a result, there was a palpable sense of drift in Indonesia on the eve of the meeting of the MPR in August 2000. Despite Wahid's fragile position and loss of parliamentary support, the consensus among Indonesian analysts was that the lack of viable alternatives made it unlikely that the MPR would oust Wahid at that time, but that Wahid could not continue with business as usual. The outcome of these pressures was Wahid's agreement to relinquish day-to-day powers to a triumvirate of the Vice President, the Coordinating Minister for Political, Social, and Security Affairs (retired Lieutenant General Susilo Bambang Yudhoyono), and the Coordinating Minister for Economy, Finance, and Industry (Rizal Ramli).[11]

This power-sharing arrangement did not prove to be viable. Wahid was not willing to share power, deepening the distrust of critics and hardening the resolve of political opponents. Wahid's political standing was further weakened in January 2001, when thousands of student demonstrators converged on the parliament to demand Wahid's resignation after a parliamentary committee report reprimanded him for his role in the scandals. On February 1, the House of Representatives (DPR) issued a memorandum of censure, the first step in a possible impeachment process. On April 30, the DPR voted overwhelmingly to issue a second memorandum, bringing the president closer to impeachment.[12]

---

[10]Many observers of Indonesian politics were critical of Wahid's dismissal of Laksamana Sukardi, regarded as one of the most honest and competent members of the administration. James Castle, chairman of the Indonesia-based consulting firm Castle Group, called it "a serious mistake of miscommunication and miscalculation." United States-Indonesia Society, Open Forum, Washington, D.C., June 15, 2000.

[11]"Indonesian icon steps in to share helm," *Wall Street Journal,* August 11, 2000.

[12]The president has one month to respond to the second memorandum of censure. If the DPR finds the president's response unsatisfactory, it can issue a third memorandum to convene a special session of the MPR for possible impeachment proceedings.

The Wahid government, or its successor, faces three critical and related challenges. The first is consolidating the country's nascent democratic institutions. The second is restarting the economy, which will be essential to political stability and democratic consolidation. The third is preserving Indonesia's territorial integrity and cohesion. These tasks will not be made easier by the differences between Wahid and Megawati on key issues such as Aceh and Irian Jaya (Papua) (Megawati supports a hard line toward separatists) and the polarization of political forces in the parliament.

THE ECONOMIC DIMENSION

Economic and Social Consequences of the Economic Crisis

The economic crisis of 1997–1998 devastated the Indonesian economy, then one of the fastest growing in the world. In 25 years prior to the crisis, per-capita income trebled and the number of people living in poverty fell sharply.[13]   Nevertheless, Indonesian banks and corporations and Jakarta's policymakers were ill prepared to deal with the regional financial crisis which began with the devaluation of the Thai baht in July 1997 and spread to Indonesia in the last quarter of that year. The legacy of the crisis was a devastated banking sector, a distressed corporate sector, and a large fiscal burden. By the fall of 2000, the exchange rate had strengthened to a midpoint between the pre-crisis rate of 3,500 rupiah to the dollar and the rate of 16,000 to the dollar when the rupiah hit bottom in December 1997, but fell again in the last quarter of the year. In January 2001, the rupiah was trading at over 10,000 to the dollar, well below the rate of 7,300 on which the government budget is based, yet providing a competitive boost to exports and enabling some reduction of the crippling fiscal deficit.[14]

The social costs have been very high. An Asian Development Bank study estimated that real earnings per worker declined by 27 percent

---

[13]International Monetary Fund, *IMF Concludes Article IV Consultation with Indonesia,* Public Information Notice No. 99/33, April 13, 1999.

[14]For an overview of the literature on the outbreak and consequences of the economic crisis in Indonesia, see Hadi Soesastro, "Implications of Indonesia's Crisis for the Asia Pacific Region: A Literature Survey," May 8, 2000, http://www.pacific.net.id/hadisusastro/000508.html.

from the pre-crisis level by the end of 1999, when inflation jumped sharply, especially in urban areas.[15] Traditional practices to help the poorest members of the community faltered as the crisis deepened. The unemployment effect of the crisis fell most heavily on youths, contributing to the aggravation of social problems and to the general breakdown of law and order.[16]

The economic crisis also widened ethnic divides in Indonesian society. Vicious rioting in Jakarta and other major cities in 1998 targeted the ethnic Chinese community. Although the riots were widely believed to have been deliberately instigated, they also reflected an endemic sense of resentment and envy held by the indigenous underclass against the economically better-off Chinese, who hold a prominent role in the economy. Anti-Chinese disturbances had been on the rise since the mid-1990s. As the Suharto regime weakened amidst economic chaos, Suharto's business links with prominent ethnic Chinese businessmen fed the resentment. The consequences of the 1998 riots on investment were the most damaging—both from the standpoint of capital flight and negative sentiment on reinvestment, a perception that holds up to the present.[17]

---

[15]James Knowles, Ernesto Pernia, and Mary Racelis, *Social Consequences of the Financial Crisis in Asia,* Asian Development Bank, Manila, July 1999. James Clad believes that the decline was steeper when measured against purchasing power and inflation. Personal communication, November 2000. A RAND study examined the impact of the crisis on the Indonesian labor market and concluded that aggregate employment remained remarkably robust through the crisis, although there was significant switching within sectors. According to the study, the drama of the crisis did not lie in aggregate employment but in real hourly earnings which, in one year, collapsed by about 40 percent for urban workers, as well as for females in the rural sector and rural males working for a wage. In contrast, real hourly earnings of self-employed males in rural areas (accounting for one quarter of the male workforce in Indonesia) remained essentially stable. The authors estimated that declines in real family incomes were about half the magnitude of the declines in individual hourly earnings, indicating that households adopted strategies to mitigate the effects of the crisis. Those strategies appear to have been most successful for those at the top of the income distribution. At the bottom of the income distribution, the crisis had a devastating impact on real incomes. See James P. Smith, et al., "Wages, employment, and economic shocks: Evidence from Indonesia," Labor and Population Program, RAND, Working Papers Series 00-07, DRU-2319-1-NICHD, October 2000.

[16]See Knowles, Pernia, and Racelis, 1999.

[17]It is estimated that up to US$20 billion in ethnic Chinese capital fled Indonesia after the anti-Chinese riots of May 1998.

The Uncertain Path to Recovery

The recovery process, such as it is, is fragile. After a sharp decline in 1998, the economy resumed a positive growth rate, accelerating to a real gross domestic product (GDP) growth rate of 4.8 percent in 2000. Nevertheless, the recovery is based on merchandise exports and government consumption and is vulnerable to shocks—domestic and exogenous. The central problems hindering a strong recovery are (1) the public and private debt overhang and (2) the inability of the Indonesian Bank Restructuring Agency (IBRA), set up in 1998 to recapitalize and restructure the banking sector, to cash out the bad debts and assets in its portfolio. These problems may be setting the stage for a relapse into recession if trade-led growth falters or oil and gas prices fall.

Most of the corporate sector is technically bankrupt, remaining in business only because, in the absence of a working bankruptcy code, the insolvent corporations have simply stopped making scheduled debt payments. Some owners have stripped their firms of assets and moved the money out of Indonesia.[18] The public sector debt has increased alarmingly and is over 100 percent of GDP, a four-fold increase from the pre-crisis level. Servicing this debt will increase pressure on the budget, already weakened by declining tax revenues and increased demands for social safety-net spending.[19]

IBRA now owns about 80 percent of the banking sector and has acquired a large stockpile of industrial assets. IBRA assets include corporate loans transferred to IBRA from insolvent banks' balance sheets; shareholder settlements—private assets of the owners of several of the banks, some of them Suharto cronies; and funds injected into banks for recapitalization. As of May 2000, IBRA had been able to collect on less than 2 percent of its 238 trillion rupiah (US$27.4

---

[18]Personal communication from Professor James Clad, November 2000.

[19]According to Indonesian economist Sjahir, the public and private debt amounts to 140–145 percent of GDP. Together with the bank debt of US$45 billion, this represents a total of 250 percent of GDP. Sjahir, USINDO presentation, January 3, 2001.

billion) on its loan book.[20] The government budget called for IBRA to collect 18.9 trillion rupiah (US$2.3 billion) by December 2000.[21]

The immobile private debt and the public debt overhang pose serious economic management challenges for the Indonesian government in the near to medium term:

• How to liquidate the assets controlled by IBRA. This is politically very difficult, given that various political factions have been fighting for control of the agency. The instability in the agency's leadership adds to the turbulence. Since the disposition of the assets controlled by IBRA will be critical to power consolidation in Indonesia in the post-Suharto era, jockeying for influence in IBRA is not likely to end soon. Nevertheless, some Indonesian analysts were hopeful that the appointment of Edwin Gerungan, a professional banker who had not been involved in politics, as the new IBRA head in November 2000 would improve transparency and reduce political interference in the agency.

• How to strike a balance between development and operational expenditures and interest payments. At the present time, about half of all projected government revenue, including the entire development component of the national budget, is going to pay interest on bonds floated to recapitalize the banks and on older sovereign obligations.[22]

• How to generate new investment. Political uncertainty has discouraged investors from returning. Despite the Wahid government's efforts to reassure the ethnic Chinese, the great bulk of ethnic Chinese capital that fled Indonesia during 1997–1998 has still not returned.

---

[20]*The Economist*, July 8, 2000.

[21]"IBRA says it might resort to fire sales," *Indonesian Observer*, Jakarta, August 23, 2000.

[22]James Clad, "Security in Southeast Asia," in William M. Carpenter and David G. Wiencek (eds.), *Asian Security Handbook 2000*, M. E. Sharpe, New York and London, 2000. Presentation by Dr. Martin Anidjar, JETRO-SAIS Conference on Business Prospects in Indonesia Under the New Government, SAIS, Washington, D.C., December 7, 1999.

- How to reconcile the pressures for decentralization and the allocation of a greater share of revenues to the provinces with the requirements to service the public debt and fund central government operations.[23]

Some of Southeast Asia's most thoughtful observers of the Indonesian scene believe that Indonesia's democratic experiment will succeed or fail on the strength of the government's economic performance. Post-Suharto governments, with severely reduced state capacity and displaying a lack of political cohesion and policy coherence, face public expectations for a rapid economic turnaround—a recipe for instability and restiveness.

On the positive side of the ledger, despite friction with the International Monetary Fund (IMF) over the pace of implementation of economic reforms, the Indonesian government managed to make headway in macroeconomic stabilization and in securing a financial lifeline from its economic partners and the international financial institutions. IMF lending, which had been suspended because of the Bank Bali scandal and the IMF's demand for the release of the full report, was restored in June 2000.[24] On July 31, 2000, Indonesia and the IMF signed another letter of intent, paving the way for the scheduled release of US$400 million. The agreement set specific targets for budget deficits, intended to lessen the impact of reduced central government revenues as the result of increased regional autonomy. The Indonesian government also undertook to take sterner measures against recalcitrant debtors and to speed up sales of government-controlled assets.[25]

---

[23]A fair amount of discussion at the Conference for Security Cooperation in the Asia Pacific (CSCAP) International Seminar on Indonesia's Future Challenges and Implications for the Region, held in Jakarta on March 8, 2000, centered on the fiscal feasibility of the Indonesian government's decentralization plan. For a more detailed discussion of this issue see Chapter Five.

[24]Presentation by Kwik Kian Gie, Coordinating Minister of Economy, Finance, and Industry, United States-Indonesia Society (USINDO), Open Forum, Washington, D.C., June 1, 2000.

[25]"Jakarta wins IMF loan with fiscal concessions to regions," *Financial Times*, August 1, 2000. For text of Letter of Intent (LOI), see Memorandum of Economic and Financial Policies, Government of Indonesia and Bank Indonesia, in IMF, www.imf.org/external/NP/LOI/idn/03. A new Memorandum of Economic and Financial Policies was signed by the new Indonesian economic team and the IMF on

On the debit side, economic management has not been viewed as competent. The chaotic state of Indonesian economic decision-making in the first semester of the Wahid government alarmed regional observers, who saw Wahid as disengaged from economic policy.[26] A new economic team composed of Wahid loyalists was put in place in the August 2000 Cabinet reshuffle. Rizal Ramli, the head of the Bulog, was appointed Coordinating Minister of Economy, Finance, and Industry, and Prijadi Praptosuhardjo, a longtime friend of Wahid, Minister of Finance. The appointments were not well received by the two largest parties in the parliament, the vice president's PDI–P and Golkar. The chairman of the parliament's Commission on Budget and Banking warned that if the new economic team did not produce results, the MPR could hold a special session, presumably to remove Wahid.[27] Wahid's move to consolidate his control of economic policy is therefore a high-risk strategy, one that will be particularly acute in the event that the newly reformulated economic team is unable to turn around the economy.

September 7, 2000. At the end of September, the IMF concluded Article IV consultations with Indonesia and determined that the country had achieved significant progress in macroeconomic stabilization. In October 2000, the Consulting Group on Indonesia agreed to provide $4.8 billion in loans to Indonesia for 2001. As of this writing, however, the IMF has not disbursed the US$400 million tranche.

[26]Discussions with Singaporean government officials and analysts on Indonesia, Singapore, February 2000.

[27]"U.S. wants market-oriented policy," *Jakarta Post,* August 26, 2000.

Chapter Three

THE EAST TIMOR CRISIS AND ITS CONSEQUENCES

The East Timor crisis was a defining event in the evolution of post-Suharto Indonesia. East Timor's separation from Indonesia and the manner in which it occurred

- Ended a 25-year policy of integrating East Timor and other outlying islands into a centrally controlled Indonesian state;

- Opened the first major crack in Indonesia's territorial integrity;[1]

- Damaged the credibility of the Habibie government at home; and

- Complicated Indonesia's relations with some of its key supporters in the international community.

The East Timor crisis was precipitated by a series of miscalculations on all sides. First, prompted in part by a letter from Australian Prime Minister Howard, President Habibie unexpectedly decided in January 1999 to hold a referendum on autonomy or independence for East Timor. Habibie took a calculated risk that the referendum would remove the East Timor issue as an irritant in Indonesia's international relations and that the pro-integrationist side would win. This, of course, was a reversal of the Suharto government stance, which had consistently refused to compromise on the issue of Indonesian sovereignty or to contemplate any special autonomy arrangement for East Timor. Habibie's call for a referendum, which reportedly was made without consulting the military or even key

---

[1]There had been a number of regional rebellions in Indonesia since independence, but none had succeeded in permanently removing Jakarta's authority.

members of his cabinet, and despite the fact that he did not have the constitutional authority to make such a decision, stunned political observers inside and outside Indonesia.

Nevertheless, the decision to hold the referendum opened the possibility of resolving an issue that had become a thorn in the side of Indonesian foreign policy. However, the fact that Habibie was proceeding without the support of other power centers in Indonesia was not a formula for success. According to a former senior U.S. official conversant with the evolution of the East Timor crisis, leading East Timor pro-independence representatives, Jose "Xanana" Gusmao and Bishop Carlos Belo, thought that the process was moving too fast, but Habibie insisted on pressing forward.

For unknown reasons, the Indonesian government made little effort to mount an information campaign to persuade the East Timorese of the advantages of autonomy within Indonesia. Instead, at some as-yet-unidentified level of the Jakarta government, a decision was made to use the "security approach" to the challenge of obtaining a "yes" vote on the referendum.[2] The months leading up to the referendum were replete with intimidation and acts of violence committed by pro-integrationist militia groups, often with police or army troops looking on without intervening.[3] (There were also reports of low-level intimidation of migrant farmers and civil servants by pro-independence elements; and some Indonesian teachers and civil servants fled East Timor in early 1999, after Habibie's announcement of the referendum.)

Referendum Day, August 30, 1999, saw little violence or interference, but once the results against autonomy were announced a week later, the militias and some military units unleashed a campaign of violence at a much more destructive level throughout East Timor. There is no question that the size of the vote against autonomy—78.5 percent in a turnout of some 95 percent of registered voters—shocked Indonesia's government and military.

---

[2]John B. Haseman, "The Misuse of Military Power and Misplaced Military Pride," in James J. Fox and Dionisio Babo Soares (eds.), *Out of the Ashes: The Destruction and Reconstruction of East Timor*, Crawford Press, Adelaide, 2000, p. 182.

[3]Harold Crouch, "The TNI and East Timor Policy," in Fox and Babo Soares, pp. 160–162.

Despite the magnitude of the stakes for Jakarta, the Indonesian government had underestimated the strength of pro-independence sentiment. Jakarta apparently believed that a combination of governmental officials and civil servants, their families, some level of support among the populace, and the pro-Indonesian sentiments of settlers from other islands would produce a close vote in favor of autonomy within Indonesia.

The outcome of the referendum was a major intelligence failure. Neither the government nor the military understood the depth of the discontent with Jakarta's rule that had simmered below the surface in East Timor for years. The violent rampage by pro-integrationist militias that followed virtually destroyed East Timor's infrastructure, forced a large part of the population to flee to the mountains or to move to the relative safety of West Timor as refugees, and seriously damaged Indonesia's international reputation.[4]

A number of theories have been advanced to explain the violence. Some can be discarded as inadequate and others may be plausible but as yet unproven. Initially, the Indonesian government claimed that the violence was the natural result of the civil conflict between pro-integrationist and pro-independence East Timorese. In fact, the Indonesians had maintained for years that the East Timorese, fractured into clans and with a history of violence even during the Portuguese colonial era, would set upon each other if the Indonesian army reduced its presence in the province.[5] But this claim is not consistent with the largely one-sided nature of the rampage by the militias. The pro-independence Falintil guerrillas by and large maintained discipline and did not attack the militias, which would have given credibility to the Indonesian forecast of political and clan violence.

There is no longer any doubt that the violence was carried out with the support of some elements of the Indonesian army, particularly

---

[4]According to press reports, some 190,000 to 300,000 people fled into the mountains during the violence, in addition to 140,000 who fled to West Timor. "International peacekeepers pour into East Timor," *New York Times*, September 21, 1999.

[5]In support of this argument, Indonesians point to the civil conflict that wracked East Timor in the wake of the 1974 Portuguese revolution and Lisbon's decision to withdraw.

elements of the Army Special Forces Command (Kopassus), which had organized and trained the militias. Some militias dated back to the 1970s, when they were formed to defend their communities against attacks by pro-independence Falintil guerrillas, provide intelligence to the Indonesian military, and serve as auxiliaries in counter-insurgency operations. Others were formed only in early 1999 after the announcement of the referendum. In many cases, the militias were augmented by outsiders, mostly from other islands in Indonesia but also from as far away as the Jakarta underworld.

One explanation posits that the High Command was unable to control the behavior of the troops in the field. The then Armed Forces Commander, General Wiranto, appeared to support this theory when he blamed "psychological factors" for the debacle. This suggested that the Indonesian military on East Timor, which included many East Timorese troops, were so committed to keeping the province that they were beyond the control of the High Command.

Another theory involves a deliberate conspiracy by the High Command to subvert the result of the referendum and keep East Timor in Indonesia, or more plausibly, partition East Timor, with the pro-Indonesian forces keeping the more economically viable areas adjacent to the West Timor border. The military's decision to unleash the violence has also been explained as an object lesson to other provinces that may have had secession in mind, or simply as retribution.[6]

The most likely, but still unproven, explanation is probably a combination of the two theories.[7] The failure of the strategy, if such it was, was made clear in the sequence of developments that led to Jakarta's reluctant acquiescence in the deployment of the Australian-led

_____

[6]The analysis of the development of the East Timor crisis described above is based on contemporary press reports; on a discussion at the United States-Indonesia Society (USINDO) Conference on East Timor, Washington, D.C., September 10, 1999, with panelists Donald K. Emmerson, Sidney Jones, R. William Liddle, and Constancio Pinto; and on a discussion at the Paul H. Nitze School of Advanced International Studies (SAIS) seminar on East Timor, Washington, D.C., September 22, 1999, with former ambassadors to Indonesia Paul Wolfowitz and Edward Masters, and Eliot Cohen, professor of strategic studies at SAIS.

[7]See Crouch and Haseman chapters in Fox and Babo Soares, pp. 160–191.

multinational peacekeeping force for East Timor (INTERFET), which meant the effective end of Indonesian rule over the half-island.

As INTERFET took control of East Timor, immediate priorities were to reestablish order, provide emergency aid, assist in the return to their homes of hundreds of thousands of displaced persons, and identify those responsible for the carnage. A key political objective— achieving Indonesian acceptance of East Timor's independence— was attained when the MPR voted in August 1999 to accept the result of the referendum. President Wahid visited East Timor on February 29, 2000, and was welcomed as a friend by the East Timorese leadership.[8]   The Indonesian government also agreed to close the refugee camps in West Timor currently controlled and used as bases by the militias, a decision that had not been implemented as of the end of 2000.

The militias that retreated into West Timor after the Indonesian withdrawal from East Timor retain the potential to destabilize the situation. These groups have interfered with the return of refugees and continue to stage raids across the border, reportedly with the concurrence of elements of the Indonesian military in West Timor. UN officials recorded 16 border incursions by militiamen during the spring of 2000. Militia attacks resulted in the death of two peace-keepers in July and August 2000. The worst incident occurred in Atambua, in West Timor, on September 6, 2000, when a machete-wielding crowd attacked a refugee compound and killed three UN workers.[9]

Australia, the United States (which provides logistical support to INTERFET), and their allies face two major challenges. One is keeping East Timor from becoming a long-term ward of the international community and allowing the eventual withdrawal of the peacekeepers. East Timor peacekeeping constitutes a significant burden on the Australian military, taking up approximately 16 percent of the country's army.[10]   There may be a question, therefore, as to how long

---

[8]"East Timor welcomes Wahid," *The Straits Times*, Singapore, February 29, 2000.

[9]"Jakarta's Shame," *Far Eastern Economic Review*, September 21, 2000.

[10]The Australian contribution to INTERFET constitutes 4,500 mostly army personnel out of the total Australian army force of 27,000. Presentation by Eliot Cohen, Johns

Australia will be willing to accept the cost and potential casualties of protracted operations. The other, related challenge, is the broader strategic problem of preventing the residual issues arising from East Timor's separation from destabilizing Indonesia and regional relations.

These considerations make a local political solution—that is, one that commits the Timorese parties to making an agreement work— essential. A strategy for stabilizing East Timor could be composed of two elements.

First, promote reconciliation between the East Timorese sides. Reconciliation will be difficult to achieve after the widespread killings and the destruction wrought by the anti-independence and pro-Indonesian forces. Nevertheless, only an arrangement that takes into account the interests of all sides is likely to produce the kind of order and stability that will permit a successful conclusion to the international peacekeeping mission. Such an arrangement, involving the pro-integrationist sector, would also help to reconcile Indonesia and the Indonesian military to East Timor's independence.

Second, there should be an international effort, led by the United States and Australia, to train and equip an East Timorese security force capable of securing the border and protecting the East Timorese population from incursion by militias based in West Timor. This program could be a much smaller version of the successful international program to train and equip the armed forces of the Bosnian Federation, which contributed greatly to stabilizing Bosnia after the failure of UN peacekeeping by restoring a balance of power between the Muslim-Croat and Serbian sides. Similarly, formation of a small but capable East Timorese security force would enhance the security of the East Timorese population, reduce the burden on international peacekeepers, and create incentives for the militias to reach a peaceful settlement.

Hopkins University Paul H. Nitze School of Advanced International Studies, Seminar on East Timor, Washington, D.C., September 22, 1999.

Chapter Four

THE CHALLENGE OF SEPARATISM AND ETHNIC AND RELIGIOUS CONFLICT

By far the most important question about Indonesia's future in the post-Suharto era is whether Indonesia will survive in its present configuration or whether it will splinter into its component parts. Other second-order but still critical issues are the prospects for Indonesia's democratic transformation and the future role of the armed forces.

The disarray in Jakarta and the separation of East Timor have encouraged secessionist movements in the economically strategic provinces of Aceh, Riau—which produces half of Indonesia's oil— and Irian Jaya (Papua), the source of an estimated 15 percent of Indonesia's foreign exchange earnings. In tandem with secessionist threats, religious and ethnic violence has been escalating in central and eastern Indonesia. The growing sectarian violence and the demands of the outlying islands for independence or greater autonomy are generating stresses that the Indonesian political system may not be able to withstand.

ACEH: THE EYE OF THE STORM

Most Indonesians view the insurgency in Aceh as the most serious challenge to the Republic's territorial integrity. Acehnese resistance to Jakarta has strong roots: First, there is the strong ethnic identity of the Acehnese. Second, the perception is widespread that the Acehnese have not benefited from the province's enormous natural wealth and that industrial development projects have been introduced merely to provide employment opportunities to outsiders, especially from Java. Third, there is resentment at the Indonesian government's policy of transmigration during the Suharto era, which

27

the Acehnese saw as a thinly veiled attempt to impose Javanese social, cultural, and economic domination. Fourth, many Acehnese reject the secular orientation of the Indonesian state, which is perceived to be at odds with Aceh's strict Sunni form of Islamic observance. Fifth, and probably most important over the last decade, there is bitterness at the Indonesian military, whose presence in Aceh has been viewed as heavy-handed, draconian, and repressive.[1]

Aceh, also known as Serambi Mekkah, "the doorway to Mecca," is, according to some historians, the region where Islam first entered both the archipelago and Southeast Asia.[2] Up until the late nineteenth century, the province had been an independent sultanate that had existed as a sovereign entity for roughly 500 years. Indeed, the Netherlands gained control of the region only after a protracted war (1873–1903) that cost the lives of some 10,000 colonial troops. Following its emancipation from Dutch rule in 1949, the newly independent and Java-based Indonesian government made a vigorous attempt to consolidate control over Aceh province, regarding it as integral to the goal of national, post-colonial unity.[3]

Acehnese disillusion with centralized rule quickly arose, however, with Jakarta generally seen as corrupt, neglectful, and "un-Islamic." Subsequent demands for autonomy—first expressed in support for the wider *Darul Islam*[4] rebellion that broke out in 1953—were partially met by Indonesia's acceptance of "special region" status for the province in 1959, which endorsed a degree of official respect for local Islamic law and custom. Nonetheless, ongoing dissatisfaction

---

[1]U.S. Committee for Refugees, "The Political History of Aceh," accessed through http://www.refugees.org/news/crisis/indonesia/aceh.htm.

[2]See, for instance, Denys Lombard, *Le Sultanat d'Atjeh au Temps d'Iskandar Muslim 1607–1636*, Ecole Francaise d'Extreme-Orient, Paris, 1967.

[3]Clive J. Christie, *A Modern History of Southeast Asia*, I. B. Tauris, London, 1996, pp. 143–144; "Dissenting History," *Far Eastern Economic Review*, July 29, 1999; "Disintegrating Indonesia," *The Sydney Morning Herald*, January 9, 1999.

[4]*Darul Islam* (literally House of Islam) is the name given to a rebellion that was launched on western Java in 1948 and that continued until the 1960s. The revolt was sparked after Islamic rebels refused to recognize the authority of the Indonesian state after the transfer of sovereignty from the Dutch in 1949 and spread from Java to north Sumatra and south Sulawesi during the 1950s. For further details, see Michael Liefer, *Dictionary of Southeast Asian Politics*, pp. 93–94.

with the secular and centralizing orientation of the New Order regime, combined with growing social and economic pressures, continued to cause unrest in portions of the province. As elsewhere in Indonesia, the central government imposed a uniform structure on villages, taking the central Java model of village organization and undermining the authority of the traditional gampong (village) heads.[5]

While most Acehnese remained uninterested in outright independence, the underlying sense of dissatisfaction in the province was exploited by a group of hard-line separatists to justify a general call to arms. Organized under the name of the *Gerakan Aceh Merdeka* (GAM), or Free Aceh Movement, the rebels initiated a low-level insurgency in the mid-1970s.[6]

GAM's "nonnegotiable" goals are the creation of an independent Islamic state of Aceh, combined with full justice for all those who have been "attacked, oppressed, and raped by the Dutch and the Indonesians."[7] Hasan di Tiro, a U.S.-educated academic descendant of the Sultans of Aceh who acted as the Aceh "ambassador" to the United Nations during the *Darul Islam* rebellion, established the organization in 1976. Although di Tiro remains the symbolic leader of GAM, he has lived in exile in Sweden since 1980, leaving responsibility for the day-to-day running of the group to Abdullah Syafei'i Dimatang, a veteran guerrilla fighter for 23 years.

Initially, GAM's operational visibility was minimal, the group suffering from a lack of active popular support and limited resources. During the latter part of the 1980s, however, GAM benefited from the provision of Libyan arms and training. This external support allowed the group to progressively escalate its activities, culminating in a

---

[5]Sylvia Tiwon, "From heroes to rebels," *Inside Indonesia,* No. 62, April-June 1999.

[6]Christie, pp. 150–156; U.S. Committee for Refugees, "The Political History of Aceh"; Federation of American Scientists, "Intelligence Resource Program: Free Aceh Movement," accessed through http://www.fas.org/irp/world/para/aceh.htm; "The Separatists," *Asiaweek*, November 26, 1999.

[7]Vanessa Johanson, "The Sultan Will be Dr. Hasan Tiro," *Inside Indonesia* No. 60, 1999, accessed through gopher://gopher.igc.apc.org:2998/OREG-INDONESIA /r.945369609.23764.55; Liefer, *Dictionary of the Modern Politics of Southeast Asia,* p. 45; "Worse to Come," *Far Eastern Economic Review,* July 29, 1999; "Giving No Quarter," *Far Eastern Economic Review,* July 29, 1999.

surge of unrest between 1989 and 1990. The response from Jakarta was stern: Aceh's special region status was terminated; the province was designated an Operational Military Zone; and the army was given a virtual free hand to crush the rebels with all means possible.

Although these measures successfully stymied immediate separatist activity, they severely strained civil-military relations and have since fueled growing radicalization and anger. By the mid-late 1990s, this brooding antipathy had, for the first time, boiled over into widespread demonstrations of support for GAM and its violent anti-Indonesian separatist agenda.[8]

Indonesian intelligence sources put GAM's current armed member-ship at between 500 and 800, although several independent analysts have estimated that its true size could be as large as 2,000.[9] Struc-turally, the group is organized along functional lines, with its forces divided into an infantry fighting battalion (overseen by a Special Command), a police force, an intelligence unit, a woman's wing, and an elite *Karades* reconnaissance squad. In addition, GAM retains a student front that is responsible for collecting community contribu-tions, running Aceh refugee camps, and organizing political propa-ganda.[10]

GAM is known to have access to pistols, automatic assault rifles, and explosives, as well as more basic armaments such as axes and ma-chetes. A series of coordinated raids carried out by the Indonesian military in 1997 showed that the group's armory was limited but cer-tainly not insignificant, with seizures during the course of one week

---

[8]Federation of American Scientists, "Intelligence Resource Program: Free Aceh Movement"; Christie, pp. 156–159; Nazaruddin Sjamsuddin, "Issues and Politics of Regionalism in Indonesia: Evaluating the Acehenese Experience," in Lim Joo Jock and S. Vani (eds.), *Armed Separatism in Southeast Asia*, pp. 111–128; "Disintegrating Indonesia," *The Sydney Morning Herald*, January 9, 1999.

[9]A rally in Bireuen regency held to celebrate GAM's 24th anniversary on December 4, 2000, was attended by 500 to 1,000 uniformed GAM troops. The security forces did not intervene, although some GAM members returning to their home district after the rally were killed in a clash with government forces in east Aceh.

[10]"Worse to Come," *The Far Eastern Economic Review*, July 29, 1999; Nisid Hajari, "Anger in Aceh," *Asia Now*, Vol. 154, No. 23, December 13, 1999; "Aceh Raises GAM Flags; Six Hurt," *The Jakarta Post*, December 5, 1999.

netting a total of 59 guns and 6,000 rounds of ammunition.[11] Aceh rebels claim that many of their weapons are procured directly from soldiers and police desperate to supplement poor pay.[12] Indonesian intelligence officials, however, suspect that most are smuggled from abroad, principally from Cambodia, via the Thai-Malaysian border area, to points along the northern Sumatra coast from Tanjung Balai, south of Medan, to Padang on the Indian Ocean.[13]

Operationally, GAM has concentrated mostly on hit-and-run attacks and ambushes directed against the Indonesian security forces, including locally based territorial troops and paramilitary police reinforcements units dispatched from Jakarta. For the most part, these attacks have been low key and sporadic, although since mid-1999 the overall scale of violence appears to have increased.[14] In common with the Islamic guerrillas in the Philippines and southern Thailand, GAM has been prepared to extend its operational focus beyond military targets, attacking Javanese migrants, suspected Indonesian sympathizers, and perceived symbols of Javanese domination. Reflecting this, more than 100 executions of suspected informers have taken place since 1998.[15] Dozens of government buildings, including schools and subdistrict administrative offices, have also been attacked or burned, forcing hundreds of civilians and government employees to flee to other parts of Indonesia.[16]

---

[11]"Islamic Separatists Held, Arms Seized," *The Australian*, February 28, 1997.

[12]Jose Tesoro and Dewi Loveard, "Aceh: Jakarta's Big Headache," *Asiaweek* 25/47, 1999, accessed through http://cnn.com/ASIANOW/asiaweek/magazine/99/1126/nat.indonesia.aceh.html. According to one commander, the going rate for these weapons can range from $220 for an FN pistol up to $15,000 for an M-16 rifle, depending on how desperate the soldiers and police are for cash.

[13]"Worse to Come," *The Far Eastern Economic Review*, July 29, 1999; "Islamic Separatists Held, Arms Seized," *The Australian*, February 28, 1997; and "Thais Run Huge Arms Trade," *The Sydney Morning Herald*, August 14, 1999.

[14]"Worse to Come," *The Far Eastern Economic Review*, July 29, 1999; "Rebel Ambush Kills Nine Police," *The Sydney Morning Herald*, May 31, 1999; "Separatists Seek Cease-fire in Indonesia's Aceh Province," *CNN Worldwide Interactive News*, January 27, 2000.

[15]In justifying the practice, one GAM rebel reportedly told a journalist, "We don't have the resources to build a prison, so our prison is in the ground."

[16]Hajari, "Anger in Aceh"; "Indonesia: Why Aceh is Exploding," Human Rights Watch Press, accessed through http://www.igc.org/hrw/campaigns/indonesia/aceh0827.htm.

In addition to armed actions, GAM has focused on inciting villagers to flee their homes for refugee camps. According to international aid officials, dozens of towns have been emptied in this way over the past year, swelling refugee sites that are thought to contain at least 90,000 people. Student committees run the camps, overseeing the provision of political and religious indoctrination. They also ensure that families are not allowed to drift back to their homes, showcasing these displaced persons as victims of military repression.[17]

GAM is not thought to benefit from substantive external operational linkages. Although the group did benefit from a certain amount of Libyan support in the late 1980s, such assistance was largely transient and was not maintained into the 1990s. Indonesian intelligence sources have speculated on the possibility of these links being reestablished in the wake of recent unrest in Aceh.[18] This is unlikely at a time when Tripoli is attempting to soften its image as an international exporter of revolution and violence.[19]

This said, external backing was not totally absent in the 1990s. GAM is known, for instance, to have received financial contributions from Acehnese businessmen in Malaysia and southern Thailand—donations that have almost certainly been used to purchase weapons from Cambodia. There have also been suggestions that militants based in Malaysia have facilitated the regional transshipment of arms. For Indonesia's generals, it is this external dimension—in terms of money and arms—that gives GAM operational significance, perhaps explaining the severity of the counter-insurgency actions that the Indonesian military were willing to contemplate during the 1990s.[20] (The international linkages of secessionist movements in Southeast Asia are discussed in more detail in Chapter 8.)

---

[17]"Captives of the Cause," *Far Eastern Economic Review*, September 2, 1999.

[18]"Indonesia: Why Aceh is Exploding," "Worse to Come," "Disintegrating Indonesia."

[19]Libya has been especially keen to validate its image as a legitimate state actor, both to normalize relations with important oil trading states such as the United Kingdom and France as well as to deflect international attention away from its alleged involvement in the Pan Am bombing over Lockerbie in 1988.

[20]"Worse to Come"; "Malaysia Denies Supporting Separatists in Indonesia," *CNN Interactive World Wide News*, July 20, 1999. In December 1999, the Indonesian Home Affairs minister publicly stated that Aceh rebels were receiving weapons smuggled from Malaysia.

PROSPECTS FOR PEACE IN ACEH

Two main factors underscore the contemporary resurgence of separatist unrest in Aceh: the continuing question of perceived economic exploitation and military excesses. Endowed with substantial reserves of natural gas and oil as well as extensive, largely underdeveloped forests, Aceh is one of Indonesia's richest provinces, accounting for between 11 and 15 percent of Jakarta's total export earnings. The Arun liquid natural gas facility in northeastern Aceh accounted for one fourth of Mobil's global revenue in the early 1990s.[21] Most of this revenue has been absorbed in the heavily populated island of Java with only 5 percent returned to Aceh in the form of central development subsidies.[22]

On its own, however, economic exploitation would probably not have been strong enough to generate overt separatist sentiments. For much of the 1980s, GAM experienced relatively little popular support, with most Acehnese merely calling for more autonomy and control over natural resources. It was only during the last decade that these sentiments began to change, largely as a result of anger generated by military excesses. One independent inquiry in 1999 catalogued no less than 7,000 cases of serious human rights violations that had occurred in Aceh since antiseparatist operations were launched a decade ago.[23] Such excesses engendered increased support for GAM and its violent separatist agenda.

The level of support for independence in Aceh is a matter of disagreement. Some Indonesians argue that the majority support union with Indonesia. Others believe that if a referendum were held, independence would carry the day. There is no question, in any event, that Acehnese sentiment is not homogeneous. For instance, Indonesian military sources point out that support for independence

---

[21]"Mobil sees its gas plant become rallying point for Indonesian rebels," *Wall Street Journal*, September 7, 2000.

[22]Donald Emmerson, "Indonesia's Eleventh Hour in Aceh," *PacNet* 49, December 17, 1999; "Too Little, Too Late," *Far Eastern Economic Review*, May 13, 1999; I Ketut Putra Erawan, "Political Reform and Regional Politics in Indonesia," *Asian Survey*, Vol. 39, No. 4, 1999, pp. 596–598.

[23]Tesoro and Loveard, "Aceh: Jakarta's Big Headache."

is concentrated in six of Aceh's 12 administrative districts.[24] Political loyalties were also colored by economic and social cleavages.[25] The Acehnese elite was solidly integrated into the Indonesian national elite. Many Acehnese occupied leading positions in the government, political parties, business, and the military in a way that few East Timorese or Papuans ever did. An Acehnese, Hasballah Saad, was appointed Minister of Human Rights in the first Wahid cabinet. Finally, GAM appears to be deeply factionalized, with cleavages among different factions and uncertain coordination between the exiled GAM leadership and the units on the field.[26]

For Jakarta, the stakes go well beyond Aceh. Many Indonesians fear that if Aceh opted for independence, Irian Jaya (Papua), East Kalimantan, and South Sulawesi would follow.[27] Therefore, few observers believe that Jakarta will offer a referendum on independence. The current Indonesian government's strategy in Aceh to address the political and economic demands of the Acehnese, short of granting independence, while conducting police operations with military support. The Wahid government and the GAM signed a temporary cease-fire (officially called a humanitarian pause) in Geneva on May 15, 2000, initially for a three-month period, and extended several times, most recently in February 2001. At the same time, the Indonesian authorities entered into direct discussion with GAM. As a confidence-building measure, Jakarta decided to withdraw combat elements of the Indonesian armed forces (TNI) from Aceh. The military did not consider the withdrawal of combat troops from the province advisable. Nevertheless, they deferred to the decision of the political leadership to turn over internal security functions in the province to the police, with the military providing backup as necessary.[28]

---

[24]Discussion with a senior Indonesian military officer, Jakarta, February 2000.

[25]In 1946, Aceh experienced a social uprising against members of the elite who had collaborated with the Dutch during the colonial period. Cribb and Brown, pp. 24–25. Cleavages between the elite and the grass roots persisted through the New Order period.

[26]Ed Aspinall, "Wither Aceh?" *Inside Indonesia*, No. 62, April/June 2000.

[27]Presentation by Andi Mullarangeng, United States-Indonesia Society (USINDO) Conference, Washington, D.C., November 30, 1999.

[28]Indonesian military sources say that the TNI becomes involved only when the police are unable to control a situation. As of December 2000, the Indonesian army was

With a cease-fire, however imperfect, in place, the Jakarta government has an opportunity to put together a package to implement its political strategy.[29] The question is whether the government's concessions will be sufficient to satisfy Acehnese demands. At present, neither the government nor the insurgents are strong enough to defeat the other, so an accommodation that permits significant autonomy for Aceh within Indonesia may be accepted as the best possible outcome by both sides.

On the other hand, the gulf between the two sides is as wide as ever. GAM hard-liners dismissed many of President Wahid's overtures as meaningless and have continued to insist that their ultimate goal of independence will not be abandoned. The group's aging exiled leader, Hasan di Tiro, has refused to put his name to the cease-fire agreement.[30] The Acehnese themselves do not appear ready to settle for autonomy, as reflected by the huge support given to an independence rally in Banda Aceh, the provincial capital, in November 1999. With crowd estimates ranging up to one million, this was the largest single demonstration of public separatist sentiment in Indonesian history.[31] That demonstration and the turnout on the same date a year later were indicative of the large pool of potential support that GAM is now able to draw on.

Most proffered solutions stress the need for the Jakarta government to make progress in three areas to gain the confidence and trust of the Acehnese:

- Greater local control, especially control of the province's economic resources. The Jakarta government will need to look seriously at implementing a meaningful and effective program of

---

pressing for the reintroduction of combat troops to Aceh. The new army chief, General Endriartono Sutarto, was quoted as saying that the police had failed in fighting separatists, and that an immediate military operation was the only way to end the bloodshed in the province. "Army wants to crush rebels as police fail," *Indonesia-News IO*, December 15, 2000.

[29]Over 400 people have been killed since the humanitarian pause was signed in May 2000.

[30]"Aceh Rebel Leader Scoffs at Jakarta Dialogue," *The Australian*, November 12, 1999; "Pausing for Peace in Aceh," *The Economist*, May 13, 2000.

[31]"Aceh Ends Wahid Honeymoon," *The Weekend Australian*, November 13–14, 1999; "Aceh's Protest Stirs Jakarta," *The Australian*, November 10, 1999.

decentralization. If the offer of autonomy is to have any relevance, people in Aceh need to be confident that regional authorities will have genuine bargaining leverage over the central administration.[32] This demand could be met through measures that have been passed or are under consideration by Parliament that would give Aceh control of 70 percent of the revenues from extractive industries and extensive local autonomy, including introduction of Islamic law for the province (see Chapter Five). The barrier, as an Acehnese political scientist noted, is a lack of trust. Given the history of Jakarta's rule in Aceh, he asked, why should the Acehnese trust Jakarta's promises?[33]

- Accountability for human rights violations by the security forces during the Suharto period. The Acehnese demand that those responsible for atrocities be held accountable for their actions and brought to justice. A process similar to the Truth and Reconciliation hearings held in South Africa could be one way to facilitate progress in this direction—an idea endorsed in 1999 by the Indonesian Attorney General, Marzuki Darusman.[34] Jakarta has tried to accommodate this demand through investigations of alleged human rights violations, which led to the trial of soldiers accused of participation in killings of civilians in Aceh. Twenty-four soldiers and one civilian were convicted in May 2000 of the massacre of 57 Aceh villagers.[35] However, the court was criticized for failing to charge any senior officers in the chain of command. The highest-ranking officer involved, a lieutenant colonel, disappeared before the legal proceeding began and has yet to be found.

- Demilitarization or at least a partial withdrawal of Indonesian troops. This step could proceed in conjunction with a compre-

---

[32]Barton, "Islam and Politics in the New Indonesia," pp. 74–75; Erawan, "Political Reform and Regional Politics in Indonesia," 606-612; Emmerson, "Indonesia's Eleventh Hour in Aceh"; "Secession's Specter."

[33]Discussion at CSCAP International Seminar on Indonesia's Future Challenges and Implications for the Region, Jakarta, March 8, 2000.

[34]"Indonesian Justice Chief Backs Truth Commission," *Washington Post*, December 20, 1999.

[35]"Indonesia convicts 25 in effort to end blood conflict in Aceh," *Wall Street Journal*, May 18, 2000.

hensive program to fully normalize Acehnese civil-military relations.[36]

Successfully achieving these objectives, logically within the framework provided by the May 2000 cease-fire agreement, would go a long way toward placating popular sentiment in Aceh, which has always tended to be oriented more toward regional justice than outright independence. More important, it would help both to consolidate the development of civilian rule in Indonesia and affirm its long-term future as a stable and key state in the heart of Southeast Asia.

The ground for an agreement, however, appears to be narrowing. With no discernible progress in the peace talks, pressure is building in political and military circles in Jakarta for a military solution to the insurgency. The military takes the view that the cease-fire only helps the insurgents consolidate their power.[37] Polls indicate strong Indonesian public support for firm government action against the Aceh rebels.[38] President Wahid's visit to Aceh in December 2000, a last-ditch effort to address Acehnese concerns and discontent and prevent an escalation of the conflict and the further alienation of the Acehnese population, had little effect, and Wahid has been under pressure to resume full-scale military operations in the province.[39]

SEPARATISM IN IRIAN JAYA (PAPUA)

Irian Jaya, renamed Papua by the Wahid government in deference to local sentiment and known by independence supporters as West

---

[36]See, for instance, Barton, "Islam and Politics in the New Indonesia," p. 74; Emmerson, "Indonesia's Eleventh Hour in Aceh"; "Secession's Specter," Op-Ed, *Asiaweek* 25/47, 1999, accessed through http://cnn.com/ASIANOW/asiaweek /magazine/99/1126/ed.aceh.html; and "Indonesia: Why Aceh is Exploding."

[37]"Aceh on the verge of all-out war," AP, December 17, 2000.

[38]74.26 percent according to a Media Indonesia poll. "Army wants to crush rebels as police fail," *Indonesia-News IO*, December 15, 2000.

[39]John Haseman, "Jakarta hardens Aceh policy: Get-tough Indonesia runs out of patience over fruitless efforts at finding peace," *Jane's Defence Weekly*, May 2, 2001. See also footnote 28.

Papua, is Indonesia's largest province,[40] comprising more than one fifth of the archipelago's total area. It contains a significant share of the country's natural resources, including the world's largest gold and copper mining operations. Run by Freeport-McMoRan Copper & Gold Inc. of New Orleans, the operations represent a $4 billion investment, with 6,000 local employees and $1.9 billion in annual revenues.[41] This area also has one of the world's largest gas fields, which is being developed by Atlantic Richfield Co., a unit of BP Amoco PLC.

Irian Jaya (Papua) was not part of the original Republic and shares few social or cultural characteristics with the rest of Indonesia. Most of the province's two million inhabitants are Melanesians living in tribes under premodern conditions and speaking some 1,000 distinct languages. When Indonesia's independence was recognized in 1949, it was agreed that the territorial status of what was then known as West New Guinea would be determined in negotiations among the colonial power, the Netherlands, and Indonesia. Sovereignty over the province was transferred to Indonesia under United Nations auspices in 1963 with the proviso that a so-called Act of Free Choice be held in 1968 to determine if the inhabitants wished to be part of Indonesia. The Indonesian authorities arranged for the Act of Free Choice to be a consultation of approximately 1,000 selected tribal leaders who met under Indonesian auspices in July-August 1969 and decided without a formal vote to confirm integration with Indonesia.[42]

Dissatisfaction with Indonesian rule, including domination of the provincial administration by outsiders, disregard for the local cultures, and exploitation of the province's natural resources under terms that did not benefit the local population created the conditions for a low-intensity insurgency led by the tribal-based Free Papua Movement (*Organisasi Papua Merdeka*—OPM). The OPM, reportedly with a hard core of some 200 fighters, does not now

---

[40]As of December 2000, the province's change of name had not yet been ratified by the Indonesian Parliament.

[41]"A pit of trouble," *Business Week*, August 7, 2000, pp. 60–63.

[42]Cribb and Brown, pp. 122–123.

constitute a serious military threat to Indonesian authority in the province, but that does not lessen the problem of local disaffection.

In February 1999, President Habibie met with a delegation of 100 provincial representatives to launch a "national dialogue." The dialogue immediately reached an impasse when the president's interlocutors declared their desire for independence. Jakarta's response was to ban all discussion or dissemination of information on independence or autonomy.[43] In May 2000, a congress of several hundred representatives from 254 indigenous tribes met in the province's capital, Jayapura, and concluded that the annexation process was illegal and that the territory was legally independent, raising a separatist flag to symbolize their stand.[44]

In the view of a senior Indonesian military officer, the insurgency in Irian Jaya is potentially more dangerous for Indonesia than the rebellion in Aceh because of the insurgents' better prospects of receiving international support. According to this view, which reflects the Indonesian experience with the international reaction to the East Timor issue, the largely Christian rebels in Irian Jaya are more likely to receive Western support than are the Muslim rebels in Aceh; in addition, the border with Papua New Guinea affords the possibility of cross-border sanctuaries for the insurgents. The OPM's low-level insurgency, however, would not be a threat to Jakarta's control if it were not for the spread and strengthening of separatist sentiment throughout the province. In many parts of the province, the Indonesian civil service infrastructure is being replaced by unofficial structures and both pro-independence and pro-Jakarta factions are organizing militias.[45]

---

[43]Nina FitzSimons, "West Papua in 1999," *Inside Indonesia*, No. 61 January-March 2000

[44]"Indonesia faces another secession threat," *Wall Street Journal*, June 6, 2000; "Papuans renew their drive for freedom," *The Guardian* (United Kingdom), July 3, 2000.

[45]As occurred in East Timor, former pro-Jakarta local leaders have joined the separatist movement. For instance, Theys Eluay, the chairman of the Papua Presidium, the pro-independence political movement, is a former Golkar legislator. Another key Presidium figure, Yorrys Raweyai, was a top official in the Pancasila Youth, a pro-Suharto paramilitary youth group. See "Indonesia faces crisis as separatism and turmoil spread," *Wall Street Journal*, November 29, 2000; "Police step up raid on Irja Rebels, Detain 47," *Indonesia-News IO*, December 3, 2000.

As in Aceh, the Wahid government first tried a conciliatory approach. It agreed to change the province's name from Irian Jaya, the name it was given after the Indonesian annexation, to Papua,[46] announced that the peaceful expression of pro-independence sentiment would no longer be punishable, released more than 60 Papuans from prison as part of a nationwide amnesty for political prisoners, and agreed to let the Papuan flag, the Morning Star, be flown as long as it was together with, and below, the Indonesian flag. Wahid also apologized for past human rights abuses, replaced hard-line military and police commanders, and kept the lines of communication open with local leaders, but ruled out any prospect of independence.[47] At the end of 2000, however, Jakarta shifted to a harder line toward separatists. The government arrested more than 50 activists, including several leading members of the Papua Presidium, the province's pro-independence political movement, and announced it would not tolerate the raising of separatist flags or other acts indicating support for independence.[48]

Whether Jakarta's alternation of concessions and suppression will succeed in keeping the province in Indonesia depends on whether the central government can deliver on autonomy and resource-sharing commitments, and whether central authority will continue to weaken as the result of stresses on the Indonesian body politic. The situation may have evolved to the point, however, where concessions short of independence may not satisfy the pro-independence sectors, which now appear to include many tribal chiefs and the provincial elite.

---

[46]The Indonesian Parliament has not yet approved the change in the province's name, so officially it remains Irian Jaya.

[47]In July 2000, Wahid met with members of a delegation of West Papuan leaders, who reported on the Jayapura congress. See West Papua Action, August 18, 2000, http://westpapuaaciton.buz.org/latest-news.html.

[48]"Jakarta arrests leaders of separatist movement in easternmost province," *Wall Street Journal*, November 30, 2000.

ETHNIC AND RELIGIOUS VIOLENCE IN EASTERN AND CENTRAL INDONESIA

Aside from separatist insurgencies, there has been large-scale ethnic and religious violence in the eastern islands of Indonesia, with the epicenter on the island of Ambon. (See Figure 4.1.) Christians used to have a small majority in the Moluccas, but the influx of Muslims from other islands has changed the ethnic and religious makeup of the region. However, at least at the onset, the conflict could not be ascribed solely to religious factors. Before the outbreak of large-scale violence, there were longstanding friendly and cooperative relations between Christian and Muslim communities in the Moluccas.[49]

Ambon city, formerly the economic hub of the Moluccas, has been effectively partitioned, with indigenous Ambonese Christians occupying one end of the town and Muslims (often transmigrants who have steadily become more important in commerce) the other. Indonesian troops guard checkpoints on the line of partition but are unable to control the militias. The violence then spread from Ambon to other islands in the provinces of Maluku and North Maluku, parts of Sulawesi, and Lombok in central Indonesia.

In November 1999, the conflict reached Ternate, the largest city in North Maluku, and Tidore, a small island south of Ternate. Dozens died when Muslims went on a rampage after a pamphlet (very likely a provocation) circulated asking Christians to rise against Muslims. Between 10,000 and 20,000 Christians and ethnic Chinese fled to Manado, a predominantly Christian city in North Sulawesi. A coalition of Christian tribes in northern Halmahera, in turn, attacked Muslims living there, and Muslims (assisted by Islamic volunteers from Java known as Laskar Jihad) launched retaliatory attacks. From the outbreak of the violence in 1999 until the middle of 2000, more than 3,000 people were killed throughout the Moluccas and more than 100,000 became refugees.[50]

---

[49]At least in Halmahera and presumably on other islands as well these relations included institutionalized mutual help arrangements. Presentation by Dr. Paul Michael Taylor, United States-Indonesia Society (USINDO), Open Forum, "Turbulent Times Past and Present in the Moluccas," Washington, D.C., September 13, 2000.

[50]Smith Alhadar, "The Forgotten War in North Maluku," *Inside Indonesia*, No. 63, July-September 2000

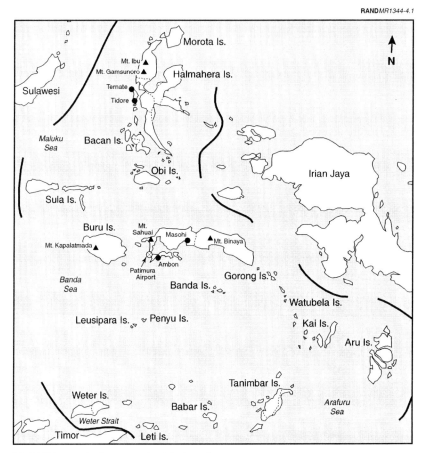

SOURCE: www.baliwww.com/maluku/map.htm

Figure 4.1—The Moluccas (Maluku and North Maluku)

Some Indonesians fear that the violence could lead to a wider sectarian conflict that could tear the country apart. Radical Muslim organizations in Java have used the violence to mobilize supporters and to attack the government for insufficient solicitude for Islamic interests. The Islam Defenders Forum, a hard-line Muslim organization, has dispatched volunteers to Ambon to fight the Christians there.[51] In the view of some Christian Indonesians, the radical Muslim agenda is to Islamicize eastern Indonesia and then extend Islamic law (*sharia*) to the whole country.[52] Laskar Jihad, in turn, has generated its Christian counterpart, Laskar Kristus ("the Army of Christ"). Some Christian leaders have organized a political movement, the Moluccas Sovereignty Front (FKM), with a view to recreate an independent South Moluccan state.[53]

There are widespread suspicions, but no proof, of military instigation of the violence. There are, however, numerous indications of breakdowns in the chain of command. Military-issued weapons were uncovered during police sweeps in Ambon.[54] Two former senior Special Forces officers were reportedly present at a riot on January 17–18, 2000, in which Muslim youths rampaged through the provincial capital of Mataram, in Lombok, in what appeared to be an organized campaign of destruction.[55] In central Sulawesi, well-disciplined units with firearms are reportedly carrying out attacks. There are reports of military desertions in West Kalimantan, where the native Dayaks turned on Madurese settlers brought in under the central government's transmigration program.[56]

Although the possibility of political manipulation cannot be discarded, the most likely trigger for the violence was the collapse of authority following the fall of Suharto, which unleashed pent-up tensions between ethnic groups and between the indigenous inhabitants and immigrants from Java and elsewhere who had moved in under the Suharto government's transmigration program.[57] Adding

---

[51]"Cry for a holy war," *Asiaweek*, January 21, 2000.

[52]Presentation by Dr. John A. Titaley, Satya Wacana Christian University, Indonesia, at United States–Indonesia Society (USINDO), Open Forum, "Troubled Times in the Moluccas," Washington, D.C., February 14, 2001.

[53]*The Economist*, March 16, 2001.

[54]Presentation by John A. Titaley, ibid.

[55]"Scene of the crime," *Far Eastern Economic Review*, January 27, 2000.

[56]Presentation by Col. (ret.) John Haseman, United States-Indonesia Society (USINDO), Open Forum, Washington, D.C., June 2, 2000.

[57]Indonesian academic Dr. Indra Samego lists the causes of the violence as follows: economic disparities between the indigenous inhabitants and migrants; religious differences; absence of state authority; and actions by provocateurs, including people

to the mix of instability were local political rivalries that had been suppressed by centralized rule from Jakarta. A subtext of the violence in North Maluku might be the rivalry between the Ternate elite and Tidore for political control of the newly established province of North Maluku. An Indonesian analyst from Ternate suggests that the attacks on Christians might have been a form of resistance to the Ternate elite, because the Sultan of Ternate (many of whose traditional retainers were Christian) was seen as siding with a Christian tribe in an incident over territorial control on the neighboring island of Halmahera.[58]

The Jakarta government's efforts to dampen the violence in the Moluccas have been ineffective. President Wahid delegated the task to Vice President Megawati, who has been singularly incapable of stemming ethnic unrest in that part of Indonesia, despite a trip to the province in the early part of 2000. The army sent reinforcements to Ambon under a transfer of command-and-control authority from the police to the regional military commander—in effect, a declaration of martial law—to little avail. In the view of most observers, military forces are too small and too thinly stretched to control the violence. There are only 16 battalions in the islands of eastern Indonesia, an area larger than the Philippines.[59] Moreover, anecdotal evidence suggests that as sectarian conflict intensifies, it affects the discipline of the troops and the integrity of the military chain of command. As a leading U.S. observer of Indonesia noted, "the government simply does not run Lombok," a statement that applies to much of eastern Indonesia as well.[60]

---

seeking to delegitimize the democratic process. Conversation with Dr. Samego, Jakarta, March 2000.

[58]Alhadar, ibid.

[59]Presentation by Indonesian Ambassador Dorodjatun Kuntjoro-Jakti, United States-Indonesia Society, Open Forum, Washington, D.C., July 21, 2000. The area referred to is presumably Kodam (Military Area Command) VIII, which includes the provinces of Malaku, North Malaku, and Irian Jaya.

[60]Presentation by James Castle, United States-Indonesia Society (USINDO), Open Forum, Washington, D.C., June 15, 2000.

"ETHNIC CLEANSING" IN KALIMANTAN

Horrific ethnic violence broke out in Central Kalimantan (Borneo) in February and March 2001. The violence involved a campaign of "ethnic cleansing" by indigenous Dayaks against Madurese migrants who had been settled in the province under the Suharto government's transmigration program.[61] The attacks involved decapitations and instances of ritual cannibalism. According to Indonesian press reports, hundreds of Madurese lost their lives in the Sampit regency and the provincial capital of Palangkaraya. Some 60,000 were displaced by violence, many fleeing to east Java.[62]

The ethnic violence in Central Kalimantan is not a new phenomenon. In 1996–1997, an outbreak of violence between Dayaks and Madurese settlers caused between 500 and 1,000 deaths in Central and West Kalimantan and led to the displacement of 15,000–20,000 people, mostly Madurese. In 1999, violence erupted again in West Kalimantan, pitting the local ethnic Malay community, supported by the Dayaks, against the Madurese.[63] The 2001 violence can be understood as the continuation and accentuation of a pattern of resistance by the Dayaks to Jakarta's policies of fostering economic development and national integration through population transfers from Java to the "underpopulated" outer islands. While Dayak leader cite cultural clashes with the Madurese as the reason for the violence, the Dayaks' animosity toward the newcomers was no doubt fueled by the economic and social marginalization of the Dayak people under the New Order. With the Indonesian security forces stretched to their limits in Aceh, Irian Jaya, and the Moluccas, there was little spare capacity to contain the seething ethnic resentments in Kalimantan.[64]

---

[61]The Dayaks are Christian or adherents of the traditional Kaharingan religion, which is a form of ancestor worship with elements of animism. They depend on slash-and-burn agriculture, hunting, and gathering for their livelihood. The Madurese come from the island of Madura, one of the poorest regions in east Java, and practice a strict version of Islam.

[62]*Jakarta Post*, March 16, 2001.

[63]"Ethnic violence and displacement in West Kalimantan (1996–1999)," in Global IDP, http://www.idpproject.org.

[64]See Peter Carey, "Indonesia's Heart of Darkness," *Asian Wall Street Journal*, March 5, 2001, for a succinct analysis of Dayak-Madurese relations.

Chapter Five

REINVENTING INDONESIA: THE CHALLENGE OF DECENTRALIZATION

No task is more formidable than managing the process of decentralization, which in the case of Indonesia involves no less than the reinvention of governance. The success or failure of the decentralization process will have a large impact on the fate of Indonesia's democratic experiment and territorial integrity.

Conceived at independence as a federated republic, Indonesia under its first two presidents, Sukarno and Suharto, developed in practice into a highly centralized state, with decisionmaking and control of the country's resources concentrated in the hands of the central government in Jakarta. Regionalist rebellions in eastern Indonesia in 1957 and in West Sumatra in 1958 were crushed,[1] and the separatist outbreaks in Aceh were suppressed, although never completely extinguished.

The new democratic forces in Indonesia have now set to reverse this state of affairs. The demand for decentralization arises because people outside of Java believe that power was not distributed fairly. The government in Jakarta has undertaken to meet this demand—to some extent because it has no choice, but also in the expectation that decentralization would lessen the provinces' distrust of Jakarta and defuse separatist sentiment.

---

[1] The rebels in eastern Indonesia adopted the Charter of Universal Struggle, or *Permesta*, which demanded a restoration of the rights of the regions, including financial autonomy, a larger share of development funds and Japanese war reparations, and some control over the appointment of government officials. Cribb and Brown, p. 78.

Law No. 22 on Regional Autonomy and Law No. 25 on Fiscal Equalization Between Center and Regions, both enacted during the Habibie administration in 1999, devolve power and revenue to the local jurisdictions. The implementing regulation devolves authority to the 30 provinces[2] and the 365 regencies *(kebupaten)* and assigns the areas of administration, public welfare, and public health as the first three areas to be decentralized, as a test before more authority is transferred.[3] Law No. 22 reverses the 1979 decision to make village governments uniform throughout Indonesia on the model of central Java and enables each province to develop its own model of village government structure, bring back old village institutions and leadership, and resolve local problems in accordance with local custom. The law gives Aceh and Irian Jaya (Papua) Special Autonomous Region status—a broader grant of autonomy that includes, for Aceh, the application of Islamic law (*sharia*) to the Muslim inhabitants, election of local officials, and compensation for past abuses by the security forces.[4]

The decentralization program entered into effect on January 1, 2001. However, government officials signaled that it would not be implemented with a "big bang," but more slowly and deliberately, to protect the delivery of services while linking the transfer of resources to the transfer of responsibilities.[5] Minister of Home Affairs and Autonomy Policy Surjadi Soedirdja stated in October 2000 that the government envisions the decentralization process as progressing

---

[2]The People's Representative Council (DPR) approved the establishment of the new province of Gorontalo, formerly part of North Sulawesi, on December 5, 2000. Since 1999, Indonesia has lost a province (East Timor); Maluku has been split into two; and the new provinces of Banten in western Java, and Bangka-Belitung in southern Sumatra were established. As of mid-December 2000, the DPR was considering establishing the islands of Riau as a separate province, an initiative opposed by the authorities in Riau province. The Habibie government divided Irian Jaya into three provinces, but this decision was opposed by the local inhabitants and had not been implemented as of December 2000.

[3]Presentation by Faisal Basri, United States-Indonesia Society (USINDO), Open Forum, Washington, D.C., July 21, 2000.

[4]Presentation by Andi Mallarangeng, CSCAP International Seminar on Indonesia's Future Challenges and Implications for the Region, Jakarta, March 8, 2000.

[5]Presentation by Rizal Ramli, Coordinating Minister for Economic Affairs, United States-Indonesia Society (USINDO), Open Forum, Washington, D.C., September 26, 2000.

through four stages: in the first stage, in 2001, the objective would be to ensure the continuity of the delivery of public services. In the second stage, during 2002–2003, the regional governments that had not implemented the decentralization program in 2001 would complete the process. The third stage, during 2004–2007, would be a period of consolidation. By the end of this period, decentralization would have been made irreversible and gaps in concepts and in the legal framework would be filled. After 2007, it is expected that regional autonomy would stabilize and improve over time.[6]

Criticism of the government's decentralization policy centered on the lack of an adequate architecture to support it. First, on the fiscal side, it was pointed out that without strengthening its revenue-collecting capability, the central government would not have sufficient funds to cover its expenditures, which include payments on an official debt estimated at over 100 percent of GDP, meet its obligations under the agreements with the International Monetary Fund (IMF), and fulfill its revenue-sharing commitments to the regions. The conundrum was that the highly centralized system of the Sukarno and Suharto eras had resulted in a large fiscal imbalance between the central government and the regions—90 percent of the revenue was collected by the central government and 10 percent by regional and local jurisdictions—but at the same time it reduced imbalances among the regions. The central government in effect functioned as an equalizer, redistributing revenue from the resource-rich to the resource-poor provinces. Decentralization would reduce the imbalance between Jakarta and the regions, but, paradoxically, increase the disparity between the richer and the poorer regions.[7]

Second, the institutional framework at the local level to manage these resources and the functions that go with them may be inadequate to the task.[8] According to a leading Indonesian decentralization expert, 30 percent of the country's regencies cannot meet the

---

[6]"Principles of Regional Autonomy Policy: Toward a Democratic and Prosperous Indonesia," speech by Minister of Home Affairs and Autonomy Policy Surjadi Soedirdja, Pre-Consultative Group on Indonesia (CGI) Meeting on Decentralization, Jakarta, October 13, 2000.

[7]Presentation by Hadi Soesastro, CSCAP International Seminar on Indonesia's Future Challenges and Implications for the Region, Jakarta, March 8, 2000.

[8]Presentation by Hadi Soesastro, ibid.

central government's standards to implement the autonomy legislation. The remaining 70 percent can meet only minimum standards. The concern of some Indonesian and foreign experts is that in the absence of transparency and accountability at the local level, decentralization could bring about corruption and the rise of "little kings" in the regions.[9]   In this regard, it is worth noting that the experience of the Philippines with decentralization was not entirely successful. According to former Philippine presidential adviser Jose Almonte, some of the unintended effects included corruption at the local level, emergence of fiefdoms, and degradation of services formerly delivered by the central government.[10]

Decentralization will probably remain a work in progress for the foreseeable future. Some degree of decentralization will undoubtedly take place—the process has built up too much momentum and the central government is too weak to prevent power from flowing from Jakarta to the regions. At the same time, central government bureaucracies remain reluctant to give up power and, as noted above, the regional and local government infrastructure may not be able to accommodate the new tasks or the public expectations that have been created. The experiences of the former Soviet Union and the former Yugoslavia are also sobering to some Indonesians, who fear that once centrifugal forces are unleashed there would be no logical stopping point.

Awareness of these risks has given the Indonesian government pause. Beginning in mid-2000, Jakarta took steps to slow the momentum of decentralization. Indicative of this trend were the August 2000 merger of the Ministry of Regional Autonomy, which had provided much of the intellectual impetus for the decentralization program, into the less hospitable Ministry of Home Affairs, and the January 2, 2001 resignation of Minister of State for Administrative Reforms Ryaas Rasyid, the leading decentralization advocate in the government. Jakarta also slowed the transfer of civil servants from the central to regional governments, and has taken steps to curb the

---

[9]Andi Mallarangeng, quoted in "Many regencies not ready for autonomy," *Indonesia-News*, November 23, 2000.

[10]Presentation by Jose Almonte, CSCAP International Seminar on Indonesia's Future Challenges and Implications for the Region, Jakarta, March 8, 2000.

ability of regional governments to borrow. On January 5, 2001, the Minister for Mines and Energy stated that the mining industry would remain under Jakarta's control for up to five years.[11]

In all likelihood, some point of equilibrium will be reached, although exactly what this will be cannot be predicted at this time. Decentralization could be key to keeping Indonesia together. Some of the more disaffected regions would not tolerate a return to Suharto-era centralization, but may be willing to be part of a state characterized by a strong measure of local autonomy. Moreover, if properly handled, decentralization would create a more favorable environment for democratic development in Indonesia by diffusing power more broadly.

At the same time, decentralization, if seriously implemented, will create a new set of winners and losers. How public opinion in populous Java reacts will be critical. There is a view that, despite its lack of commodity exports, Java will fare well under a decentralized system because of the concentration of agricultural and industrial resources on the island. On the other hand, centralizing tendencies might reassert themselves (as they did in the early 1950s) if the Javanese see themselves on the losing side of the ledger, or if central government leaders perceive the process as accelerating rather than retarding separatist tendencies.

---

[11]"Chaos Rebuffed," *Far Eastern Economic Review,* January 18, 2001.

Chapter Six

THE MILITARY IN TRANSITION

ORGANIZATION, MISSIONS, AND CAPABILITIES

The Indonesian military, known as ABRI (*Angkatan Bersenjata Republik Indonesia*—Armed Forces of the Republic of Indonesia) under the New Order and renamed TNI (*Tentara Nasional Indonesia*—Indonesian National Military) in 1999 is arguably the only institution that cuts across the divisions of Indonesian society. The Indonesian armed forces are approximately 300,000 strong, of which 235,000 are in the army, 47,000 in the navy, and 21,000 in the air force. In addition, the National Police, which was part of the armed forces until its separation in April 1999, numbers about 180,000. The army has long been the dominant military service, although the Suharto government's military modernization plans (abandoned after the onset of the economic crisis) focused on improving air and naval capabilities.

There are 17 operational commands, of which 13 are army commands. Two of these commands are particularly important because of their location in or near Jakarta and their striking power. One is the Army Strategic Reserve (*Kostrad*), which was Suharto's power base in his rise to power in 1965–1966. *Kostrad* numbers 35,000 and is described as a "strategic striking force." It comprises two infantry divisions, one headquartered in Jakarta and the other in Malang, in east Java, with three airborne brigades and three conventional infantry brigades. The other is the Army Special Forces (*Kopassus*), headquartered in Jakarta, with a strength of 6,000 to 7,000. *Kopassus* troops are trained in intelligence gathering, special operations techniques, and airborne and seaborne landings; they played a prominent role in counterinsurgency operations in East Timor and else-where. The rest of the army is deployed in 11 territorial commands or Kodam.

The air force has two operational commands (*Ko-Ops*). *Ko-Op* I, headquartered in Jakarta, is responsible for operations west of Jakarta; and *Ko-Op* II, at Ujungpandang, South Sulawesi, for opera-tions east of Jakarta. The navy maintains two operational naval commands (the eastern and western fleets), a Military Sealift Command, and a marine corps with two combat infantry regiments, one stationed in Jakarta and the other in Surabaya.

As an archipelagic country with 17,000 islands and a coastline of 55,000 kilometers—more extensive than the entire European coastline—Indonesia is dependent on its navy and air force to maintain inter-island communications and transport troops and military stores. See Figure 6.1.

The navy, with 17 main frigate-size combatants, 57 corvettes and patrol boats (including 16 unseaworthy former East German corvettes), 26 landing craft that can carry 200 troops, 13 mine countermeasures craft (mainly used for coastal patrol), and two German T-209/1300 submarines, is deployed in what are considered to be key sea-lanes or sensitive areas, such as the Strait of Malacca, the waters west and southwest of Sumatra, and the Makassar Strait. More recently, the navy is attempting to seal off violence-torn islands in the Moluccas. The navy also has some naval air capabilities, including anti-submarine warfare and search and rescue helicopters.

The air force, in addition to its territorial defense mission, conducts strategic surveillance of the waters around Indonesia, transports ground forces and equipment, and carries out humanitarian relief missions. Combat aircraft include one squadron (12 aircraft) of F-16A/Bs, based at Madiun-Iswahyudi air base, in Java; two squadrons (24 aircraft) of BAe Hawk Mk 109/209 and one squadron (13 aircraft) of Hawk Mk 53 light-attack aircraft based at Supadio air base, in Pontianak, West Kalimantan, and at Ranai, on the island of Natuna; one squadron (12 aircraft) of upgraded F-5E/Fs; one squadron (20 aircraft) of refurbished A-4Es operating out of Pekan Baru, in central Sumatra, and Ujungpandang; and one reconnaissance squadron of 12 OV-10F aircraft. The air force also operates two squadrons of C-

130s with 19 aircraft and a number of smaller transport and rotary-wing aircraft.[1]

Military modernization plans and readiness were devastated by the economic crisis in Indonesia. The air force and the navy, more dependent on access to technology and spare parts than the army, were disproportionately affected. In June 1997, the Suharto government canceled plans to purchase seven F-16As and two F-16Bs—originally

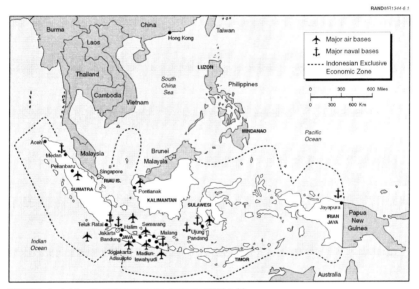

SOURCE: *Jane's International Defense Review*, September 1997, p. 34.

Figure 6.1—Major Indonesian Military Bases

[1]Sources for the above description of the Indonesian armed forces are Brian Cloughley, "Indonesia fights domestic diversity," *Jane's International Defense Review*, September 1997, pp. 33–34; Takashi Shiraishi, "The Indonesian Military in Politics" unpublished paper 1998, p. 3; numbers are from *The Military Balance, 1998/99*, pp. 181–183, the Periscope data service, http://www.periscope.ucg.com; and personal communications from Col. John Haseman (USA, ret.).

built for Pakistan—because of congressional criticism of Indonesia's record on human rights and East Timor. Indonesia subsequently announced plans for the acquisition of 12 Russian SU-30MK and eight Mi-17 helicopters, but suspended them after the onset of the economic crisis.

Since then, the Indonesian air force budget fell 50 percent in U.S. dollar terms and the number of flight hours dropped by almost one half. Moreover, the impact of the budgetary cutbacks was amplified by restrictions on the sale of U.S. military equipment and spare parts to Indonesia. Owing to the lack of funding and spare parts, most of the vessels in the Indonesian navy are in varying states of disrepair and only half of the F-16s and C-130s in the air force inventory are operational.[2]

The national budget is not the only source of income for the military, of course. The military derives significant (if undetermined) funds from commercial activities and military-linked foundations. According to press reports, a military foundation like *Kartikas Eka Paksi* controls 26 companies and the army's Cooperative Center, *Inkopad*, at least 12.[3] In private discussions, Indonesian military leaders deplore the military's reliance on commercial activities for funding, but argue that in order to pay the salaries and maintain the standard of living of the troops there is no alternative as long as insufficient funds are allocated to the armed forces in the state budget.

THE TERRITORIAL SYSTEM AND THE DUAL FUNCTION

The Indonesian armed forces had their origin in the fighting units organized in 1945 to defend the newly proclaimed Republic of Indonesia from the Dutch.[4] They were used against the Islamic fun-

---

[2]This discussion of the condition of the Indonesian air force is based on discussions with senior Indonesian air force officers in Jakarta in March 2000.

[3]Kyrway Report 2000-6, "Analysis of the Political Situation in Indonesia," October 2000, http://www.gtzsfdm.or.id.

[4]See Tjokropranolo, *General Sudirman: the leader who finally destroyed colonialism in Indonesia*, Australian Defence Studies Centre, Canberra, 1995.

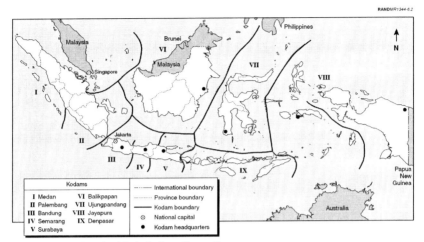

SOURCE: Federation of American Scientists Intelligence Resource Program.

NOTES: Jakarta has its own Kodam known as Jaya. There is also an unnumbered Kodam at Ambon. Boundary representation is not necessarily authoritative.

Figure 6.2—Military Area Commands (Kodam)

damentalist guerrillas of *Darul Islam* in the early 1950s,[5] against the provincial rebellions in 1957–1958, and against the Communists in 1965. From its experience during and after the war for independence, the military developed a doctrine of "total people's defense and security" (*hankamrata*) and, as noted above, a territorial command structure of 11 territorial commands (*Komando Daerah Militer*—Kodam), each responsible for the defense of a part of the archipelago.

The doctrine contemplated mass mobilization to fight invaders and to support operations against internal enemies. Kodam I covers Aceh, northern Sumatra, and Riau; Kodam II, southern Sumatra; Kodam III, west Java; Kodam IV, central Java and the Special Region of Yogyakarta; Kodam V, east Java; Kodam VI, Kalimantan; Kodam VII, Sulawesi; Kodam VIII, Irian Jaya; Kodam IX, Bali, the central Indonesian islands of Nusa Tenggara, and Timor; and Kodam Jaya (not numbered), Jakarta. A newly established unnumbered Kodam

---

[5]Literally "House of Islam." These were Muslim guerrillas in west Java who fought against the Dutch and later the Republic.

with headquarters at Ambon, covering the Moluccas, is the eleventh Kodam. See Figure 6.2.

From a political perspective, the key territorial commands are Kodam Jaya and III, each with an infantry brigade, because of their importance to Jakarta's security.

Each Kodam is divided into Korem (*Komando Resor Militer*), headed by a colonel. Korems, in turn, are divided into military districts or Kodim (*Komando Distrik Militer*), headed by a lieutenant colonel, and districts into subdistricts or Koramil (*Komando Rayon Militer*), with non-commissioned officers in charge. This territorial structure, which reached down to the village level, constituted in effect a parallel structure to the civil administration. All levels have an intelligence function, and all levels above the subdistrict command have an intelligence staff providing operational intelligence to the commander and reporting directly to the national-level military intelligence agency.[6]

The structure dovetails with the military's internal security mission. It was designed to allow the military to be close to the people, deprive potential rebels of support, and enforce Jakarta's authority. In a statement to the parliament, a former commander in Aceh stated that there was not a day that he did not visit Muslim schools and meet with the *ulama* and local leaders to remind them of the national outlook, of the national ideology, *Pancasila*, and of the authority of the central government.[7] Under the New Order, the territorial system was used to maintain Suharto in power and monitor the activities of religious organizations, student organizations,

---

[6]Shiraishi, p. 3. After the abolition of the Agency for the Coordination of Support for National Stability Development (*Barkostanas*) in March 2000, two intelligence agencies remained: the Strategic Intelligence Agency (BAIS), responsible exclusively for military intelligence, and the State Intelligence Coordinating Board (BAKIN). In the fall of 2000, the Wahid government was reportedly considering the reorganization of the intelligence community, including the replacement of BAIS with separate service intelligence agencies and the establishment of a Defense Intelligence Agency under the Ministry of Defense. Kyrway Report 2000-6, "Analysis of the Political Situation in Indonesia," October 2000, http://www.gtzsfdm.or.id.

[7]Cited in United States-Indonesia Society, "Indonesia's Military," p. 24.

trade unions, and other non-governmental organizations that could become sources of dissident activity.[8]

The military's heavy involvement in politics was justified by the concept known as *dwifungsi* or dual function. This concept gave the military a sociopolitical function and an institutionalized role in government. The military had corporate representation in the parliament and active and retired military officers served in positions in the Cabinet, the civil administration, and state corporations. As retired general and Ambassador Hasnan Habib noted, the dual function was practiced since 1945, driven by the demands of the revolution and the war for independence, in which the armed forces carried out a political as well as a military struggle.[9] It was officially formulated by General Nasution in a speech in 1958, and Suharto used it to turn the military into a political pillar of the New Order.

CIVIL-MILITARY RELATIONS FROM SUHARTO TO WAHID

As an institution, the military remained neutral in the events that led to the fall of Suharto, the Habibie interregnum, and the election of Wahid.[10] Nevertheless, as even senior Indonesian officers acknowledged, the military suffered a severe loss of reputation and credibility as the result of its association with the Suharto regime. The military's reputation also suffered from its involvement in the rampage by the pro-Indonesia militias in East Timor. The TNI responded to the pressures for change by retreating from its political role and undertaking a revision of its doctrine. So far the changes have amounted to a revolution in civil-military relations. The most important changes are:

* Abandonment of the *dwifungsi*. Under the new dispensation, the military still has a sociopolitical role (*peran*), but it is no

---

[8]Presentation by Harold Crouch, ibid.

[9]A. Hasnan Habib, "The future of the Indonesian armed forces," paper delivered at CSCAP International Seminar on Indonesia's Future Challenges and Implications for the Region, Jakarta, March 8, 2000.

[10]There was, however, a fair amount of intrigue centering around alleged plotting by Suharto's ambitious son-in-law Lieutenant General Prabowo Subianto and his supporters.

longer viewed as a separate function from defense. Military representation in the Parliament was reduced from 75 to 38 and is scheduled to the phased out by 2004.[11]

- Separation of the police from the armed forces.

- Severance of ties to the former ruling party, Golkar.

- Appointment of Indonesia's first civilian Minister of Defense (Juwono Sudarsono)[12] and of a non-Army officer (Admiral Widodo) as commander-in-chief of the armed forces.

- Requiring military officers appointed to nonmilitary government positions to retire from active duty.

Civilian control of the military became a front-burner issue in the wake of the suspension of General Wiranto from his job as Coordinating Minister for Defense and Security and the shake-up in the TNI command in February 2000. In discussions with Indonesian interlocutors in Jakarta at the time of Wiranto's dismissal, all of the Indonesians agreed that President Wahid was in control of the military and that there was little danger of a coup. One political analyst thought that Wahid dismissed Wiranto "to break the myth of Army power."[13] Another maintained that Wahid had fired Wiranto in response to external pressure and that Wiranto was not an issue in domestic politics or with the military.[14] Singaporean analysts posited that Wahid was simply exercising the time-tested divide-and-conquer methods that Suharto had employed in his time to consolidate control of the military.[15]

---

[11]In its August 2000 session, the MPR transferred the military seats from the DPR to the MPR, effective from 2004 to 2009.

[12]Juwono had been governor of the National Resilience Institute (*Lemhannas*), the military's institute of higher studies, and had close links to the reformist wing of the TNI. He suffered a stroke in January 2000, which hindered his effectiveness. He was replaced by another civilian, Professor M. D. Mahfud, in August 2000.

[13]Conversation with Indria Samego.

[14]Conversation with Soedibyo.

[15]This was a widely shared view in Singapore. According to a Singaporean expert on the Indonesian military, Wahid moved against Wiranto because he was the most vulnerable target. Wiranto had risen as a result of his relationship with Suharto, whom he had served as military aide de camp and did not have a strong personal following in the TNI.

The issue of democratic civilian control of the military is somewhat more complicated than a matter of an elected president's ability to reshuffle the high command. At no point in Indonesian history— except possibly in the aftermath of the failed 1965 coup—has the military threatened the control of the political elites. Suharto thoroughly dominated the military during his long reign. General Leonardus Benjamin ("Benny") Murdani wielded great power in the military during his tenure as armed forces commander (1983–1988) and Minister of Defense and Security (1988–1993), but was not able to prevent his own removal and a large-scale purge of his supporters.

Under Murdani's successor, Feisal Tanjung, there were frequent personnel reshuffles in the military, each involving large numbers of senior officers. On one level, these changes accorded with a number of structural requirements, such as the need to correct the imbalance between the number of senior officers and the number of upper-level positions and to expand command opportunities for younger officers. At the same time, the frequent command changes prevented the consolidation of power centers that could challenge Suharto's authority.[16]

Some Indonesians argue that the real danger in civil-military relations is that external political interests might politicize the military.[17] The issue, then, is less the military developing a political will independent of the civil authorities than political sectors seeking military alliances or using promotions and assignments to secure the military's support. President Wahid's role in the Wiranto affair raised concerns for this very reason. Wiranto's removal from his position as Coordinating Minister of Defense and Security in March 2000 also involved the transfer of 74 commanders and staff officers in a reshuffle reminiscent of the Suharto era.[18] Healthy civil-military rela-

---

[16]Shiraishi, pp. 5–9. Shiraishi examines the careers of General Wiranto and LTG Susilo Bambang Yudhoyono, two rising stars in the 1994–1998 period, and notes that neither served longer than 15 months in a senior command position. By contrast, Suharto's son-in-law, Prabowo Subianto, spent over four years with the Special Forces, which was regarded as his power base and where he reportedly retains influence.

[17]United States-Indonesia Society, "Indonesia's Military: Backbone of the Nation or Achilles' Heel?" *Proceedings of USINDO Workshop*, March 28, 2000, Washington, D.C., p. 5.

[18]The reshuffle included the controversial appointment of outspoken reformer LTG Agus Wirahadikusumah to the key position of Kostrad commander.

tions, as a senior Indonesian officer noted, require not only that the military obey the civilian authorities but that in military affairs the civilian authorities respect the military's procedures and chain of command.

The stresses in Indonesian civil-military relations have given rise to frequent rumors of coups. Is a coup a realistic concern? The consensus of Indonesian military experts is that, short of a catastrophic political event, the armed forces will not stage a coup. In the first place, the TNI does not speak with one voice. There are divisions between traditionalists and reformers, and even among the reformers themselves. Moreover, the military is too dispersed and Indonesia is too vast for a military commander or clique to take over. An attempted coup would likely split the armed forces along its fault lines with unpredictable consequences.[19]

The real problem with civilian control of the military is the weakness of the chain of command. The greater the distance from the capital, the more Jakarta's authority becomes attenuated. Cross-border raids into East Timor by pro-Indonesian militias with military ties—even as Wahid was visiting East Timor to apologize for Indonesian behavior—brings into question the extent of Jakarta's control over military units in the provinces.[20] Therefore, command reshuffles do little to address the real issues of civilian control. Effectively institutionalizing civilian control of the military would require depoliticizing decisions on military assignments and promotions,

---

Wirahadikusumah was replaced in August 2000 in connection with an effort by a politically weakened Wahid to placate other TNI factions on the eve of the MPR meeting. Wirahadikusumah appeared sidelined for good in August 2000 after Defense Minister Mahfud accused U.S. Ambassador Gelbard of intervening with Wahid in favor of Wirahadikusumah and after 46 Army generals threatened to resign if he were appointed to replace Gen. Tyasno Sudarto as army chief of staff. Kyrway Report 2000-6, "Analysis of the Political Situation in Indonesia," October 2000, http://www.gtzsfdm.or.id.

[19]Retired BG Soedibyo pointed out, for instance, that a successful coup would require the cooperation of the commanders in Jakarta, East Java, West Java, South Sumatra, and the Strategic Reserve. Discussion in Jakarta, March 2000.

[20]Presentation by Harold Crouch, United States-Indonesia Society (USINDO), at USINDO Conference on the Indonesian Armed Forces; see also "Indonesian Militias Target U.N. Forces in East Timor," *Washington Post,* August 12, 2000. Prabowo is suspected of stirring the pot in Timor because of his connections with the Special Forces, who were involved in organizing and arming the militias.

combined with a stronger effort on the part of the civilian authorities to demarcate clearer boundaries between the political and military spheres, and a gradual phasing out of the territorial command structure.

DOCTRINAL CHANGE IN THE TNI

The TNI is in the process of what could be its most important doctrinal change since independence. According to senior TNI officers, the TNI's goal is to shift from its traditional focus on internal security threats to a focus on external defense. This shift has been under way since the early 1990s, when the military's conventional warfighting capabilities were enlarged with the acquisition of early warning systems and light attack aircraft, but came to a halt with the onset of the economic crisis.

Indonesian officers do not foresee a large-scale conventional external military threat in the near future. More likely, they anticipate that there will be low-intensity threats, such as piracy, border clashes, encroachment on Indonesian maritime resources, and possibly the spillover of a conflict involving third parties. Territorial disputes with Malaysia and with Vietnam over the demarcation of the continental shelf are also regarded as potential flashpoints. It is to these areas, they believe, that the thrust of the TNI's focus and resources should be directed in coming years.[21]

The intention of the military reform is to transfer internal security functions to the newly separated national police. According to the new doctrine, the police are to develop paramilitary capabilities to deal with insurgencies and large-scale internal security threats. If the police cannot handle a situation, the TNI would come to their assistance, but only at the direction of the central authorities.

Some Indonesian officers suggested that this policy is already being implemented in Aceh. However, civilian defense experts maintain that the TNI is still heavily involved in counterinsurgency operations in Aceh and Irian Jaya (Papua). Although under the new doctrine the

---

[21]Discussion with staff of the National Resilience Institute (Lemhannas), Jakarta, March 2000.

military may not have the legal responsibility for internal security, it may not have a choice in situations where the territorial forces are the only ones available.[22]

TNI leaders agree that there is a duplication of functions between the military's territorial structure and civilian regional administrations and acknowledge the need for change. Lieutenant General Agus Wirahadikusumah expressed the radical reformist view most forcefully, in a statement before the parliament in March 2000 in which he demanded the abandonment of the territorial structure. Not everyone in the TNI, however, agrees that the territorial structure should be abandoned. Senior military officers as well as civilian officials agree that in many rural areas of Indonesia the civilian governmental infrastructure is inadequate or nonexistent and therefore the territorial system in these regions must remain in place until an adequate civilian government presence can be established. Some army officers believe that the police are incapable of taking on the internal security functions that traditionally have been performed by the military. They argue that the military needs to keep the territorial structure in place to be able to project the presence of the central government in the villages, which they maintain is essential to preventing conflict among ethnic and religious groups.

In between the radical reformist and the conservative view is the argument for gradual change, which is the prevailing view in the TNI.[23] At the closing ceremony of a seminar on the TNI territorial role at TNI headquarters in Jakarta in January 2001, Lieutenant General Agus Widjojo, TNI Chief of Territorial Affairs and considered a moderate reformer, said that the territorial role was acceptable as long as it was restricted to national defense.[24]

---

[22]Discussion with Indra Samego.

[23]This analysis is based on discussions with senior active and retired Indonesian military officers. Professor Harold Crouch notes that if the territorial system were abandoned, it would be necessary for the police to take over some of the internal security functions of the territorial system. However, the police number fewer than 200,000, while estimates of the numbers needed for a country of Indonesia's size range up to 600,000. United States-Indonesia Society, "Indonesia's Military," p. 10.

[24]"Agus Wijoyo: TNI Territorial Role Still Needed," *Indonesia-News JKPT*, January 25, 2001.

According to a senior Indonesian military officer, there are cultural as well as doctrinal changes within the TNI. Under Suharto, he explained, the emphasis was on outcomes. Methods and process were not important as long as the results were satisfactory. Now that Indonesia is launched on a democratic experiment, the military is expected to focus not just on finding the quickest and most effective way to deal with a problem, but to consider the means as well as the ends. This would require the TNI to display greater sensitivity to human rights and develop the capability to operate effectively within a transparent democratic order.

Over the short term, doctrinal change has generated a great of deal of uncertainty and confusion in the TNI. Some officers complain that contradictory demands are being placed on the military. They are expected to maintain order, they say, but their hands are tied. One officer noted the inability of the national police to enforce the laws against separatists—he cited, in this respect, the police's failure to prevent the lowering of the national flag at a separatist meeting in Irian Jaya or the occupation of government buildings by protesters— or safeguard security force outposts from rebel attacks.

Implementing the new doctrine will require enormous changes in the TNI's organizational structure, training, and personnel practices. It would also require resources that are not currently available to reequip the Indonesian armed forces.

Chapter Seven

ALTERNATIVE INDONESIAN FUTURES

Indonesia's future will be shaped by the strategic choices made by the country's principal political actors as they confront the tensions generated by the breakdown of the old order. There are tensions among new political actors and forces trying to sort out new power relationships; between Jakarta and the periphery—never fully suppressed under Suharto's New Order and fueled by a resentment of Javanese centralism and exploitation; between the indigenous population and ethnic Chinese; between Muslims and religious minorities; between moderate and radical visions of Islam, within the Muslim majority; and between different conceptions of the military's role in society. Table 7.1 outlines a number of possible futures.

DEMOCRATIC CONSOLIDATION

An electoral process in 1999 that delivered a government with a claim to legitimacy and popular support increased the likelihood of democratic consolidation. The best-case scenario involves the evolution of civil-military relations on a model of democratic civilian control.[1]

---

[1]Another view questions the assumption that the Western model of democracy and civil-military relations is the best suited for Indonesia. According to this view, a heavier hand, though tied to genuine democratic electoral legitimization of government, is the best formula to preserve Indonesia's unity. This argument goes to the core of the question of the suitability of Western-style democracy to non-Western societies. This broad subject cannot be done justice in a footnote, the authors take the view that democratic consolidation in Indonesia would advance U.S. geopolitical as well as humanitarian objectives, that Indonesians themselves are striving to maintain a democratic form of government, and that the possibility that they may not be successful is not an argument for not supporting Indonesian democracy, with the

Some promising signs are apparent in this regard. The Indonesian military is committed to divesting itself of its formal role in politics. It is transferring internal security functions to the newly separate police and developing a new military doctrine with a focus on external defense. For the first time, civilian defense ministers have been appointed and an officer from a service other than the army became armed forces commander.

Table 7.1

Possible Paths of Indonesian Political Development

Scenario	Domestic Political Consequences
Democratic consolidation	Could provide more favorable environment for peaceful resolution of ethnic/religious conflict
Aborted transition and political breakdown	Greater likelihood of increased strife and/or military takeover
Military rule. Variants: a. Turkish model: limited military rule with eventual return to civilian government b. Pakistani model: military alliance with radical Islamic forces c. Burmese model: repressive open-ended military rule with support of military-controlled political front	Consequences will depend on the variant of military government: Model a is likely to be more stable than other variants because of its limited goals and duration. Models b and c would be more difficult to sustain and could give way to a radical Islamic takeover or influence or disintegration scenarios
Return to authoritarian civilian rule	Could be a disguised military rule. Not likely to be stable in post-Suharto environment
Radical Islamic influence	Could involve shift from secular to more visible Islamic orientation. Probably resisted by the military, unless the military itself splits or is overwhelmed by radical forces
Disintegration	Could be overt or de facto within a nominally unified state. Could come as the result of any of the downside scenarios listed above

caveat that a policy adjustment may be necessary if Indonesia's democratic experiment fails.

For the present, the civilian government's position with the military appears to be relatively secure, but the course of civil-military relations in Indonesia is by no means settled. President Wahid, during his first year in office, focused on consolidating his authority over the senior military leadership in Jakarta, but the weakening of his political position also weakened his hand vis-à-vis the military. The military appears to have made a distinction between loyalty to the president and loyalty to the Constitution—for instance, the army leaders reportedly refused to support a bid by Wahid to declare a state of emergency in February 2001, at the time when the parliament was debating the motion of censure. Beyond the power struggles in the capital, there are questions on the extent to which the authorities in Jakarta control powerful regional interests, particularly outside of Java.

The best-case scenario presumes that the political leadership in Jakarta will move the political reform process toward a stable democratic order; it is also contingent on whether the government will be able to get a grip on the economy, restore investor confidence, and bring about some improvement in the standard of living of ordinary Indonesians. If the Wahid government or its successor were able to manage these challenges successfully, the prospects for democratic consolidation would improve.

The current trend lines, however, do not appear to be encouraging. As of the end of 2000, the governing coalition had all but unraveled. President Wahid has seen the erosion of his support in Parliament and survived in his position only through the tolerance of Vice President Megawati's PDI–P. The economic recovery, such as it is, is fragile. According to sources in Singapore, some of the ethnic Chinese capital that had fled Indonesia returned after Wahid's election, but the flow of capital slowed because of lack of confidence in the Indonesian government's economic management.[2]

In addition, there are a number of wild cards that could derail the process. One is the government's handling of the insurgencies and separatist movements, particularly in Aceh and Irian Jaya. The best outcome in Aceh would be a political settlement through which Aceh

---

[2]Discussion with analysts in Singapore, February 2000.

remains part of Indonesia, but with substantial autonomy and a fair share of the province's revenues from its natural gas resources. If the Jakarta government's efforts to conciliate the Acehnese fail, its options would be to concede independence to Aceh as it did to East Timor, which would be unacceptable to many Indonesians, especially those in the military, or to prosecute a difficult and costly war.

If Aceh separates, the question becomes whether Aceh's independence will intensify separatist sentiment in other parts of Indonesia. Would Irian Jaya, Sulawesi, and East Kalimantan follow Aceh's example? What would be the impact on the Moluccas, where what amounts to an ethno-religious civil war is under way? Violence in a disintegrating Indonesia could certainly spread to other parts of the country and could generate unsustainable strains on the military and the political system. The latter option—prosecuting the war against separatists—is equally problematic, given the TNI's shortfalls in equipment and resources and its tarnished image, and the likely international backlash against the effects of a large-scale counter-insurgency effort.

Beyond demands for outright separation, the Jakarta government faces a significant political challenge in managing the demand on the part of the provinces, especially outside Java, for greater autonomy and control over local resources. The government has responded by passing laws, that devolve power and revenue to the local governments. In the view of some, only Indonesia's transformation into a federated state can over the long run save the country from disintegration.

On the other hand, dismantling the old centralized state represents an enormous challenge. As previously noted, the experience of the Philippines with decentralization was not entirely successful. In Indonesia, the risks are even greater. Decentralization, if not managed carefully, could reduce the central government's ability to fund essential functions, create greater imbalances between resource-rich and resource-poor provinces, and accelerate disintegration.

ABORTED TRANSITION AND POLITICAL BREAKDOWN

With the political balance in Indonesia and the challenges confronting the Jakarta government discussed above, it would appear that the probability of a stable democratic transition is not high. The issue is whether the political turbulence that would attend the possible near-term transition to a post-Wahid government would be severe enough to derail Indonesia's democratic evolution.

How this scenario might unfold would depend to a great extent on the modality of the transition to a post-Wahid government—an acrimonious impeachment would be far more destabilizing than a resignation—and on Megawati's political skills. At the time of his election, Wahid was widely regarded as better qualified by temper and political philosophy to promote national conciliation and cohesion than any alternative. By and large, the confidence in his inclusive approach has been justified, but he has been unable or unwilling to impose order and coherence on his administration. The resulting sense of drift has retarded the resumption of investment and economic recovery and has eroded Wahid's parliamentary support.

Vice President Megawati has great legitimacy. Her party, PDI-P, received the largest number of votes in the 1999 parliamentary election. Nevertheless, Megawati did not play a significant role in the first year of the Wahid presidency, despite a power-sharing arrangement negotiated with Wahid at the August 2000 MPR meeting. According to her critics she has not demonstrated the leadership skills and vision to lead Indonesia in this time of turbulence.

If Wahid were to disappear from the scene, either through physical incapacitation or removal by the MPR, the most likely outcome would be continued instability. Continuation of unstable conditions and weak governments in Jakarta would impede economic recovery and foster the growth of alternative power centers. A post-Wahid government headed by Megawati would likely be less conciliatory toward separatist movements and autonomy-seeking provinces; the outcome could be an escalation of the fighting in Aceh and other provinces. Political instability and economic deterioration amidst disintegrating central control and ethnic and religious strife in parts of Indonesia would create an environment favorable to the growth of authoritarian movements and radical Islamic parties.

Under this set of conditions, the best scenario that can reasonably be expected would be for the Indonesian government to muddle through until the election of a new president in 2004. Alternatively, there could be a breakdown of central authority. A breakdown scenario could involve a collapse of authority in Jakarta, with different factions vying for power. One subscenario could be an attempt by radical Islamic parties to change the secular character of the Indonesian state. Another subscenario could involve the gradual loss of central control over parts of the periphery and the secession or attempted secession of outlying provinces. Violent disintegration could provoke demands for international humanitarian intervention—that is, from Jakarta's perspective, a repeat of the East Timor experience. The military, which views itself as the guardian of the country's territorial integrity and political stability, would see no option but to reinsert itself into politics.[3]

VARIANTS OF MILITARY RULE

Unlike Pakistan or Turkey, where the military has regularly stepped in to redress perceived failures of civilian government, there is no tradition of military coups in Indonesia.[4] Over the short term, therefore, only a catastrophic political failure—for instance, the breach of the constitution or impending dismemberment of Indonesia—could compel the military to assume control of the government. Should that occur, one could envisage a military government of two basic variants:

The first would be a military-technocratic government that preserved the balance between the secular and Islamic ("Green") factions in the TNI; economic policymaking would be in the hands of nonpolitical

_____

[3]An early warning sign is when senior military officers call on political leaders to put aside personal interests and unite to act in the national interest, as Army Commander General Sutarto reportedly stated at an address to the Staff and Command College in Bandung. "Army Chief lashes out at bickering politicians," *Indonesia-News JKTP*, November 17, 2000. The governor of the National Resilience Institute (Lemhannas), the Indonesian armed forces' higher studies institute, warned on November 22, 2000 that Indonesia could break up if no actions were taken to defuse economic and political instability. "Lumintang: Indonesia in danger of collapsing," *Indonesia-News JKTP*, November 22, 2000.

[4]The obvious exceptions, of course, were the failed 1965 Communist-backed coup, organized by Sukarnoist junior officers, in which six senior generals were murdered, and Suharto's "rolling coup" against Sukarno during 1965–1967. The latter was a direct consequence of the former.

technocrats. This would be the most moderate variant of a military-led government and probably one that would become more attractive as the situation deteriorated.

The second would be an alliance of the military with one of the political sectors, possibly one or more of the Islamic parties. This variant would be closer to the Pakistani model. It would also be the most dangerous because it would exacerbate ethnic and religious tensions and accelerate the disintegration process. Some observers are troubled by the Pakistani mix of military rule and support for radical Islamic groups and are concerned about the possibility of the same mix occurring in Indonesia.[5]

In either case, a military-led government would be inherently unstable because the military would likely face the opposition of important sectors of domestic public opinion and the international community. Moreover, such a government would probably lack the political tools and experience to run a country as large and diverse as Indonesia. Over time, a military government would widen fissures within the military itself as the different military factions competed over the distribution of power and policymaking authority.

The Pakistani model military-led government could evolve, in the next phase of Indonesia's political development, in any of three directions: (1) Restoration of civilian government. There would be political and financial pressure from the international community for the military to restore civilian rule. Some elements in the Indonesian military would also want to move in this direction. The military, on the other hand, would be unlikely to transfer power to civilians until some of the issues that led to the takeover had been addressed. (2) A more repressive form of military rule—what could be called the "Burmese" model. The military could take this track if it becomes convinced that Indonesia's survival was at stake and that firm measures were required to maintain its territorial integrity.[6] (3) Disintegration and political radicalization. The military could simply

---

[5] M. D. Nalapat, "Historic chance for RI's military," *Jakarta Post,* March 3, 2000.

[6] It is interesting to note that the Indonesian military's political role served as an ideological inspiration for the Burmese generals' drive for political power. See "Burma's generals want Indonesian-style politics," *Far Eastern Economic Review,* August 17, 1995.

crumble in the face of pressures it could not withstand. If combined with the upsurge of radical Islam, this could lead to what, for lack of a better name, could be called the "Iranian scenario."

WORST-CASE SCENARIOS: RADICAL ISLAMIC RULE AND DISINTEGRATION

A radical Islamic takeover in Indonesia should be considered a low-probability scenario at this stage. Militant Islamic parties captured only 6 percent of the vote in the 1999 elections—14 percent if the votes received by Amien Rais' Islamic Mandate Party (PAN) are added. President Wahid's National Awakening Party (PDB), the political arm of the traditionalist Nahdlatul Ulama organization, received 12 percent, and the Islamic United Development Party (PPP), established as an official religious party under Suharto's New Order, 11 percent. By contrast, the PDI-P and Golkar, parties representing the secularist tradition of the Indonesian state, received more than 50 percent of the vote.

Radical Islamic parties, therefore, represent only a minority of Indonesian Muslim opinion. Moreover, a bid to change the secular status of the Indonesian state is likely to be opposed by secularists in the political establishment and the military. That said, the religious war in the Moluccas and a sense that Jakarta authorities have failed to protect Muslim interests have led to an upsurge in Islamic militancy. Radical Islamic militias, particularly in eastern Java, have engaged in violent suppression of what they consider un-Islamic activities.[7] Although, we reemphasize, at this point a radical Islamic takeover would appear to be a low-probability event, it can not be excluded in an environment of political disintegration and institutional decay. Under some circumstances, a militant minority could succeed in neutralizing institutional resistance and enforcing its views on the moderate but passive majority.

Disintegration could be the end stage of some of the downside scenarios described above. Weak governments and chaotic conditions would accelerate the development of alternative power centers in Indonesia's outer islands. As the center becomes less relevant, the

---

[7]"In Indonesia, radical Islam makes waves," *Wall Street Journal*, December 11, 2000.

incentives for resource-rich areas such as northern Sumatra, Sulawesi, and Irian Jaya (Papua) to acquiesce in a subordinate economic and political relationship with Jakarta would decrease. Regional powerholders could consolidate control with local military collaboration, as in the 1950s, and sovereignty could arrive almost as an afterthought.[8]

Disintegration could also come about as the result of a split in the military, which conceivably could fracture along some of the many divides in Indonesian society. It could follow the outbreak of large-scale violence in Java and secessionist or dissident challenges in the outer islands that the thinly stretched military is unable to control. A scenario in which Indonesia's status as a secular state was endangered could also accelerate the secession of the non-Islamic areas in eastern Indonesia.

It is difficult to predict how far the process of disintegration will go should it begin. The obvious candidates for separation from Indonesia are Aceh and Irian Jaya (Papua), but there could be more. An independent Aceh could be a model or pole of attraction for other provinces in Sumatra. Kalimantan and Sulawesi have the mass, population, and resources to constitute viable states. In the Moluccas, the communal and religious violence has not led to the emergence of a full-fledged separatist movement in the Christian-majority areas, but this could change in a disintegrating Indonesia, particularly in the event of the separation of neighboring Irian Jaya (Papua). The regional consequences of this and other scenarios are discussed in the next chapter.

PROBABLE OUTCOMES

Indonesia's prospects for the short to medium term (one to three years) are for a continuation of weak governments and worsening of security conditions in provinces experiencing separatist or communal violence. Although there is a fragile (and perhaps short-lasting) economic recovery under way, as discussed in Chapter One, political conditions deteriorated in the second half of 2000. The Wahid gov-

---

[8]The authors are indebted to Dr. James Clad for this view of disintegration. Personal communication, January 2001.

ernment survived its first years in office, but with a narrowing political base and under an ever-present threat of impeachment. If, as many observers expect, Wahid resigns or is removed from office, Vice President Megawati will succeed to the presidency in accordance with the Constitution. Islamic objections to the elevation of a woman to the presidency appear to have been somewhat muted, at least for the time, but a Megawati succession would not necessarily bring in greater stability.

Over the longer term, therefore, barring a lasting upturn in the economy or a workable agreement with disaffected provinces, the odds may be better than even for one or more of the downside scenarios described previously to come to pass. This prognosis, of course, assumes a linear progression of the trend lines described in the preceding chapters. There is potential for a negative outcome even sooner if there is a political downturn in Jakarta or a major misstep by the Indonesian leadership in dealing with any of the country's multiple crises.

Chapter Eight

REGIONAL CONSEQUENCES OF INDONESIAN FUTURES

Indonesia's evolution could drive the Southeast Asian security environment in either of two directions. A successful democratic transition in Indonesia—to the extent that the Jakarta government retains the benign orientation toward Indonesia's neighbors established under Suharto—would be factor of stability in Southeast Asia. It could lead to the reconstruction of a Southeast Asian security system grounded on democratic political principles. A stable Southeast Asia, in turn, would translate into reduced opportunities for potential Chinese hegemonism and, by the same token, could facilitate China's emergence as a more powerful state without destabilizing the regional balance of power.

How Indonesia handles the tensions arising from ethnic and religious diversity, human rights, and political participation could also provide a model for other ethnically and religiously diverse countries in Southeast Asia and beyond. In its foreign policy orientation, a democratic Indonesia could be expected to continue to play the role of the good international citizen, seeking a stable international order and strong relations with its major economic partners and with neighboring ASEAN states.[1] For the United States, a stable democratic Indonesia would offer better prospects for bilateral and multilateral cooperation, particularly full normalization of military-to-

---

[1]Anthony L. Smith points out the elements of continuity in Indonesian foreign policy from Suharto to Wahid, in "Indonesia's Foreign Policy Under Abdurrahman Wahid: Radical or Status Quo State?" *Contemporary Southeast Asia*, Vol. 22, No. 3, December 2000. Some of these core elements would continue to shape the direction of a democratic Indonesian government's foreign policy.

military relations, by reducing the salience of human rights concerns in the bilateral relationship. That said, a common commitment to liberal democracy does not preclude conflicting interests. Politics in a democratic Indonesia—to the extent that it accommodates nationalist or anti-Western forces, for instance—could well drive Indonesian policy in directions that the United States might find uncomfortable.[2]

The downside scenarios—political deterioration, a return to authoritarian or military rule or, in the worst-case scenario, disintegration—would drive the regional security environment in the opposite direction. Southeast Asia would become more chaotic and unstable, less inviting for investment and more prone to capital flight, and more vulnerable to a bid for regional domination by a rising China. The likely consequences of some possible scenarios are sketched in Table 8.1.

Of the possible downside scenarios, a return to authoritarian or military rule could have the least severe consequences, from the standpoint of regional stability. An authoritarian or military government would likely be inward oriented, preoccupied with issues of domestic stability, and supportive of the regional status quo. The emergence of an authoritarian or military regime would not foreclose an eventual return to a democratic civilian government, but probably not before a degree of stability was restored. A turn toward authoritarianism in Indonesia could provoke an adverse reaction by the United States, the European Union, nongovernmental organizations (NGOs), and other members of the international community concerned about political and human rights in Indonesia. If this were to occur, the government in Jakarta could seek countervailing alliances with other authoritarian states. Despite historic suspicions of

---

[2]The idea that Indonesia should forge a common front with other Asian powers in contraposition to the West has always had currency in Indonesia. After his election, President Wahid proposed a Jakarta-Beijing-New Delhi "axis," a concept he subsequently downplayed, but that some commentators interpreted at the time as a revival of Sukarnoist foreign policy principles.

Table 8.1

Regional Consequences of Indonesian Scenarios

Scenario	Regional Consequences
Democratic consolidation	Increased regional cooperation and stability Decreased opportunities for Chinese hegemonism Better prospects for security cooperation with the United States Strengthening of democratic tendencies in ASEAN
Return to authoritarian or military rule	Strengthening of authoritarian tendencies in ASEAN Decreased cooperation with U.S. and Western countries and institutions concerned with political and human rights; possible U.S. and international sanctions Possible rapprochement with China
Radical Islamic influence	Alignment with radical Middle Eastern states and movements on international issues Support or encouragement of Islamic separatists in Mindanao and southern Thailand and of Islamic political forces in Malaysia Increased isolation of Singapore Anti-Western foreign policy orientation
Disintegration	Increased potential for intervention by outside powers Increased refugee flows Increased piracy and transnational crime Severe regional economic dislocation Diminished effectiveness of ASEAN

Beijing's intentions, an authoritarian Indonesian regime may find compelling reasons for a rapprochement with China. Such a development, in turn, could open insular Southeast Asia to expanded Chinese influence, isolate the Philippines, and put pressure on Singapore to abandon its cooperative security relationship with the United States.

It can also be expected that a military regime would be supported by most of the other ASEAN states, which are likely to be more concerned about stability than democracy in Indonesia. Some say that the region would secretly welcome it, especially if it stops disintegration and the sense of disorder in Jakarta and other major cities. Therefore, sanctions or pressure by the United States and other extraregional powers on Jakarta for a rapid return to democracy would not be supported by regional states and could widen cleavages between the United States and ASEAN as a whole.

A government in Jakarta dominated or influenced by radical Islamic elements would be far more disruptive of regional and international security and stability than the preceding scenario. Indonesia could be expected to draw closer to radical states and movements in the Middle East and join the forces opposing an Israeli/Palestinian peace agreement, the sanctions on Iraq, and the U.S. and Western presence in the Persian Gulf. Regionally, Jakarta could become a focus for the export of Islamic radicalism to the rest of Southeast Asia. An Islamic upsurge in Indonesia would encourage separatists in Mindanao and the southern Philippines, and could have a significant impact on Malaysia, where the Islamic Party of Malaysia (PAS) has made inroads in traditional strongholds of the ruling United Malay National Organization (UMNO).

The political system in place in Malaysia over the last 30 years—a multiethnic coalition dominated by UMNO—is under pressure as the result of the generational and political divisions manifested in the downfall, trial, and imprisonment of former Deputy Prime Minister Anwar Ibrahim. This system could find itself under renewed assault by a surging PAS aligned with rising Islamic political forces in Indonesia.

An alignment of Islamic parties and forces in Indonesia and Malaysia would be unsettling to the ethnic Chinese in both countries and to the city-state of Singapore. Singapore, wedged between these two Malay-majority countries and dependent on international trade for its economic survival, would find political instability and, in particular, ethno-religious conflict in its two immediate neighbors threatening. The Singaporeans are very much aware of the need to work with friendly countries to deal with threats to regional stability. At the same time, they are also aware of the limits of their influence, particularly in dealing with Indonesia's enormous problems, and of the danger that any perceived intervention in Indonesian affairs could backfire by stoking Indonesian nationalism and anti-Chinese sentiments.[3]

_____

[3] Discussions with Singaporean government officials and defense analysts, Singapore, February 2000.

Indonesian disintegration would have severe humanitarian and economic consequences. First, one can assume that disintegration would be accompanied by large-scale violence in the Indonesian archipelago. There would be increased refugee flows, probably to Malaysia, Singapore, and Australia. An increase in piracy and transnational crime can be expected, brought about by economic dislocation and the breakdown in law and order. There would be few, if any prospects of the return of investment capital to Indonesia, and the rest of the region—even well-ordered economies like Singapore—would suffer by association. Progress toward the development of a serious ASEAN Free Trade Area (AFTA) would slow, as would the integration and rationalization of transport and infrastructure in the region.

A deteriorating regional environment could also place at risk Philippine democracy, which steadily strengthened after the fall of the Marcos regime in 1986. Since then, there were three successive democratic presidential elections, democratic civilian control of the military was strengthened, and former military coup-makers and guerrillas alike were incorporated into the political system. Despite the impressive achievements of Filipino democracy, strong political and economic threats to stability remain. After his abortive impeachment on bribery charges, Estrada was driven from office in January 2001 by a military-backed popular uprising. The new government of President Macapagal Arroyo has to contend with significant Communist and Islamic insurgencies and the disaffection of Estrada's supporters.[4]

Instability or disintegration would strengthen centrifugal forces elsewhere in Southeast Asia. The impact of the emergence of mini-states in the former space of Indonesia could be especially threatening to regional states confronted by ethnic and religious divisions. As Indonesians point out, the rebellion in Aceh, although deriving from local sources, is not an isolated phenomenon. It is linked to a series of Muslim insurgencies of varying degrees of intensity, from southern Thailand to the southern Philippines.

---

[4]As of the beginning of February 2001, Estrada maintained that he was still the legitimate president of the Philippines. Estrada is believed to retain substantial support among the poor, who constituted his core constituency in the 1998 election.

Muslim separatists in the Philippines are believed to maintain links with fundamentalist Islamic organizations in a number of other countries, including Pakistan, Egypt, and Afghanistan, and to have developed regional networks with radicals in Malaysia and insurgents in Aceh and southern Thailand.[5] Thai authorities believe that Muslim separatists in southern Thailand received backing from Islamic militants in Malaysia, with the sanction of the ruling Islamic Party (PAS) in the province of Kelantan.[6]

Malaysia's role vis-à-vis Muslim separatism in the Philippines and Thailand is difficult to pin down. The Malaysian External Intelligence Organization, which operates out of the Prime Minister's office, runs a serious intelligence operation from Sabah, maintaining links through Muslim groups anchored in the immigrant Malay community and the Melanau Muslim coastal people, to Philippine Muslim rebel groups. These go back to the Moro National Liberation Front (MNLF) links in Sabah during the 1970s. The extent to which Malaysia has it within its power to cut off support to the Muslim separatists in the Philippines is problematic. Turning against co-religionists in the southern Philippines is unpopular in UMNO circles, and Kuala Lumpur resents Manila' inability to abandon territorial claims to Sabah. On the other hand, brazen kidnappings of visiting tourists in Sabah by Abu Sayyaf rebels infuriated the Malaysian government and led to shakeouts in the Sabah intelligence operation.[7]

There are well-established arms pipelines from Cambodia through Thailand and Malaysia that serve Muslim insurgents in Aceh and Mindanao, the Tamil Tigers in Sri Lanka, and Sikh separatists in India. The Patani United Liberation Organization (PULO), a Muslim separatist organization in southern Thailand, is reportedly involved in arms smuggling to the Acehnese guerrillas.[8]

Muslim insurgencies in Aceh, Mindanao and the Sulu archipelago, and southern Thailand derive sustenance from the socioeconomic

---

[5]See "The Moro Insurgency," in Chapter Nine.

[6]See "Muslim Separatism in Southern Thailand," in Chapter Nine.

[7]Personal communication from Dr. James Clad, January 2001.

[8]"Worse to come," *Far Eastern Economic Review*, July 29, 1999.

and political grievances of the Muslim population in these countries, and some base their claims to legitimacy on the revival of the rights of Islamic states and sultanates that formerly held sway in their respective regions. Islamic separatists reject the legitimacy of the modern Southeast Asian states and the regional status quo—an orientation that could make for unpredictable behavior toward regional and international institutions and norms, should they come to power in their areas. "Rogue states" in the area could interfere with fragile regional maritime commerce patterns. As Donald K. Emmerson noted, countries for which the Malacca Strait is a lifeline would wonder how an independent state of Aceh would regard freedom of navigation.[9] The next chapter examines in greater detail separatist movements in the Philippines and Thailand.

---

[9]Donald K. Emmerson, "Indonesia's Eleventh Hour in Aceh," *PacNet Newsletter*, No. 49, December 17, 1999.

Chapter Nine

MUSLIM SEPARATIST MOVEMENTS IN THE PHILIPPINES AND THAILAND

THE MORO INSURGENCY

Separatist violence in the southern Philippines centers around the activities of the Moros,[1] the Muslims on the islands of Mindanao and the Sulu archipelago that have historically constituted a stronghold of Islam in Southeast Asia. Four main factors underscore Moro separatist sentiment. First is fear of having religious, cultural, and political traditions weakened (or possibly destroyed) by forced assimilation into a Catholic-dominated Philippine Republic. Second is resentment of Catholic transmigration from the north. This has not only dispossessed many Muslims of what are considered to be ancient and communal land rights, it has also reduced the Moro population to a minority in their own homeland. Third is frustration with Mindanao's lack of economic development. Currently, 15 of the Philippines' poorest provinces are located in the south, which additionally has the country's lowest literacy rate (75 percent) and life expectancy (57 years).[2] Fourth is a tradition of warlordism, banditry, and blood feuds.

Ever since the Spanish colonization of the Philippines in the mid-1500s, governments in Manila have aimed at both political domination and religious conversion in Mindanao. An integral part of this

---

[1]Spanish for "Moors," a term sixteenth-century Spaniards extended to Muslims in the Philippines and elsewhere.

[2]Peter Chalk, "The Davao Consensus: A Panacea for the Muslim Insurgency in Mindanao?" *Terrorism and Political Violence,* Vol. 9, No. 2, 1997, pp. 80–83.

effort has been transmigration, something that was particularly evident during the early 1900s when Christians from other parts of the Philippines were encouraged to settle in the south. These programs altered the ethnic and religious balance in Mindanao—from an overall Muslim majority in Mindanao and the Sulu archipelago at the end of the nineteenth century to less than 17 percent of the population today—and precipitated bitter conflicts over land distribution and ownership. These demographic changes engendered a deep sense of resentment that has since been compounded by integrationist policies that have largely ignored local cultural, religious, and political traditions.[3]

Exploitative economic policies and uneven investment flows, which have mainly benefited industries in the northern Philippines, have exacerbated disparities between Catholics and Muslims, further fueling perceptions of local alienation and deprivation.[4] It is against this sociopolitical and economic context that the separatist Islamic insurgency in the southern Philippines has been fought since 1971.

The Moro National Liberation Front (MNLF), the largest of the Moro armed organizations, which historically served as the main focus for armed Islamic resistance to Manila in the southern Philippines, made peace with the Philippine government in 1996.[5] The agree-

---

[3]Muslims retained a majority in some parts of their traditional territory—for instance, the Sulu archipelago remains predominantly Muslim. Michael A. Costello, "The demography of Mindanao," in Mark Turner, R.J. May, and Lulu Respall Turner (eds.), *Mindanao: Land of Unfulfilled Promise*, New Day Publishers, Quezon City, Philippines, 1992, pp. 40–41. See also R. J. May, "The Wild West in the South: A Recent Political History," in Turner, May, and Respall Turner, p. 128; Daniel Lucero, "The SPCPD: A Breakthrough Towards Peace," *Office of Strategic Studies (OSS) Digest* (July/August 1996), p. 5; and Dynamic Research and Media Services, *A Study of the New Developments on the MNLF Secession Movement in Relation to AFP Plans*, Office of the Deputy Chief of Staff for Plans, Quezon City, Philippines, 1989, p. 2.

[4]Islam, "The Islamic Independence Movements in Patani of Thailand and Mindanao of the Philippines," *Asian Survey*, Vol. 38, No. 5, May 1998, p. 452.

[5]The MNLF was founded by Nur Misuari, a Tausug, in 1971. The group defined itself according to three main beliefs: First, that the Moro people constitute a distinct *bangsa* (nation) that has a specific Islamic historical and cultural identity. Second, that the *bangsamoro* have a legitimate right to determine their own future. Third, that the MNLF has both a duty and obligation to wage a *jihad* against the Philippine State. For further details, see Mark Turner, "Terrorism and Secession in the Southern Philippines: The Rise of the Abu Sayyaf," *Contemporary Southeast Asia*, Vol. 17, No. 1,

ment established the Autonomous Region of Muslim Mindanao and gave MNLF a stake in the Philippine political process. Two separatist groups remain active in the southern Philippines: the Moro Islamic Liberation Front (MILF) and the Abu Sayyaf Group (ASG).

The MILF was formally established in 1980 as a splinter movement of the MNLF. The group is far more religiously oriented than its parent movement, emphasizing the promotion of Islamic ideals rather than the simple pursuit of Moro nationalist objectives.[6] The avowed political objective of the MILF according to its leader, Hashim Salamat, is the creation of a separate Islamic state in all areas where Muslims are a majority in the southern Philippines.[7] The essential purpose of this polity, to be known as the Mindanao Islamic Republic (MIR), is to establish a system of government that upholds and applies s*haria* (Islamic law) in all aspects of daily life. Such a goal is to be achieved through a combined strategy of *da'wa* (Islamic preaching) and *jihad* (holy war).[8]

According to Philippine National Police (PNP) and military intelligence estimates, MILF's current strength is between 8,000 and 11,000, although some independent analysts have put the total num-

---

1995, p. 10; P. B. Sinha, "Muslim Insurgency in the Philippines," *Strategic Analysis*, Vol. 18, No. 5, 1995, p. 638; and A. Misra, "Guerrillas in the Mist," *Pioneer*, July 11, 1994.

[6]Indeed, the original incorporation of "Islamic" in the group's name was a deliberate move designed to set the organization apart from the more secular orientation of the MNLF.

[7]These areas are defined as central Mindanao, parts of the Zamboanga peninsula, Davao, Basilan, Sulu, Tawi-Tawi, and Palawan.

[8]"The Moro Islamic Liberation Front (MILF)," unpublished paper prepared for the Philippine National Intelligence Coordinating Agency (NICA), p. 5; Alfredo Filler, "Muslim Militancy: A New Threat to Security and Stability, a Philippine Viewpoint," unpublished paper prepared for the Armed Forces of the Philippines, July 1995, p. 20; Concepcion Clamor, "Terrorism in the Philippines and Its Impact on National and Regional Security," paper delivered before the CSCAP Working Group on Transnational Crime, Manila, May 1998, p. 8; "Held to Ransom," *Far Eastern Economic Review*, May 25, 2000; "Rumble in the Jungle," *The Australian*, March 23, 1999; Sheikh Abu Zahir, "The Moro Jihad," *Nidal'ul Islam* 23, April-May 1998, p. 11; "Commissar of the Faith," *Far Eastern Economic Review*, March 23, 1996; "Crescent Moon Rising: The MILF Puts Its Islamic Credentials Upfront," *Far Eastern Economic Review*, February 23, 1995; and "Rebels Without a Pause," *Asiaweek*, April 3, 1998.

ber of fighters as high as 15,000.[9] MILF fighters are organized into a military wing known as the Bangsamoro Islamic Armed Forces (BIAF), which is composed of at least six separate divisions. The troops are trained mostly by veterans of the Afghan war and rotated through the organization's 13 major camps. All of these were linked to the MILF's central headquarters at Camp Abubakar until its capture by the Philippine army in July 2000.[10]

Traditionally, most of the MILF's violent activities have taken the form of orthodox guerrilla warfare with hit-and-run attacks directed against the Philippine military. Generally speaking, the group has not emphasized indiscriminate violence against civilian and noncombatant targets. Such "self-restraint" has been used to distance the MILF from the activities of the Abu Sayyaf Group and is very much in line with the group's own self-image as a revolutionary military (as opposed to terrorist) force.[11] Nonetheless, terrorist-type tactics have been periodically used against Christian communities, employees of companies who have refused to pay "revolutionary taxes," or local government and police officials.[12]

Abu Sayyaf (literally, "Bearer of the Sword") is a self-styled fundamentalist insurgent movement whose birth can be traced to 1989.[13] In 1999, the Armed Forces of the Philippines (AFP) Southern Command estimated Abu Sayyaf's overall support base at 1,148, with a regular armed component consisting of approximately 330 fight-

---

[9]The MILF, itself, claims an armed membership of 150,000. See Mike Winchester, "Mindanao," *Soldier of Fortune*, September 1998, p. 66; "Philippine Left Announces Ties with Islamic Rebels," *CNN Interactive World Wide News*, March 29, 1999.

[10]Correspondence with Philippine National Police Directorate for Intelligence, Camp Crame, Manila, June 1998. See also Anthony Davis, "Islamic Guerrillas Threaten Fragile Peace on Mindanao," *Jane's Intelligence Review*, Vol. 10, No. 5, May 1998, pp. 32–33; and "Rebels Without a Pause," *Far Eastern Economic Review*, April 3, 1998.

[11]Clamor, "Terrorism in the Philippines," p. 8; Filler, "Muslim Militancy," p. 20.

[12]See, for instance, "A Hostage Crisis Confronts Estrada," *The Economist*, May 6, 2000; "Philippine Officials Link Bombings to Muslim Rebels, as Third Hostage-Taking Unfolds," *CNN Interactive World Wide News*, May 3, 2000; and "Military Finds 2 Beheaded by Philippine Rebels," *Washington Post*, May 7, 2000.

[13]The group's original name was the *Mujahideen* Commando Freedom Fighters (MCFF). The MCFF renamed itself first the *Jundullah* (literally, "Servants of Allah") in 1992 and then the ASG in 1993. The group is also occasionally referred to as the *Al Harakat Al Islamiyya* (AHAI).

ers.[14] The group is governed by an Executive Committee headed by a *Caliph* and eight other religious leaders. Together these constitute the so-called *Minsupala* Islamic Theocratic State Shadow Government (MIT-SG).[15] Abdurajak Janjalini represented the supreme power within the organization until he was killed in a shootout with the police in December 1999. Since then the group has been effectively leaderless, although its members have stated their determination to regroup under a new *Caliph* as soon as a suitable successor can been found.[16]

In terms of revolutionary political violence, virtually all of Abu Sayyaf's activities are terrorist in nature. In March and April 2000, the group abducted 50 elementary school teachers and children on the island of Basilan and took 21 hostages, including foreign tourists, at a diving resort in Malaysia. At the time of writing, 31 hostages had been released, four had been beheaded, and another 15 rescued by the Philippine military.[17]

The overall objective of Abu Sayyaf is the establishment of an independent and exclusive Islamic state in Mindanao. Whereas the MILF merely aims for independence, the Abu Sayyaf additionally espouses violent religious intolerance, advocating the deliberate targeting of all southern Filipino Catholics. Abu Sayyaf also sees its objectives in Mindanao as intimately tied to an integrated effort aimed at asserting the global dominance of Islam through armed struggle and an

---

[14]Correspondence with PNP Directorate for Intelligence, Camp Crame, Manila, June 1998.

[15]Clamor, "Terrorism in the Philippines," p. 5; Filler, "Muslim Militancy," p. 16; "Briefing on Terrorism," briefing paper prepared by the Philippine National Intelligence Coordinating Agency (NICA), January 1996, pp. 6–9.

[16]See "Abu Sayyaf to Regroup, Gov't Warns," and "Kidnappings to Continue in South," *The Philippine Daily Inquirer*, December 22, 1998.

[17]"A Hostage Crisis Confronts Estrada," *The Economist*, May 6, 2000; "Philippine Military Begins Assault on Muslim Rebels," *CNN Interactive World Wide News*, April 22, 2000; "Philippine Forces Hit Rebel Stronghold," *Washington Post*, April 24, 2000; "Gunmen Take Foreigners Hostage in Malaysia," *Washington Post*, April 25, 2000; and "Military Finds 2 Beheaded by Philippine Rebels," *Washington Post*, May 7, 2000.

extreme religious fervor not generally shared (at least overtly) by the MILF.[18]

Ethnic identification tends to underlie support for the different insurgent groups. The Tausugs, the politically dominant group in the Sulu archipelago, backed the MNLF. The bulk of the MILF's members come from the 1.6 million Maguindanaoan tribe (who are scattered throughout central Mindanao), the 1.9 million Maranaos (a trading community from Lanao del Sur), and the Iranos from North Cotabato and Basilan. Most of Aby Sayyaf's active backing is concentrated in Zamboanga, Basilan, and Sulu (where the Abu Sayyaf's main training camp is situated). However, pockets of residual support are also thought to exist throughout the southern Philippines, notably in the poverty-stricken regions of western Mindanao. The majority of the group's members are Muslim youths, with many of the older cadres reportedly veterans of the Afghan war.[19]

Both the MILF and the Abu Sayyaf Group are thought to retain and benefit from well-established links, both regionally and internationally. Intelligence sources within the Philippines believe that MILF leader Salamat maintains close relations with *ulamas* (many of whom were his classmates at Cairo's Al-Azhar University) heading fundamentalist Islamic organizations in a number of other countries, including Pakistan, Egypt, and Afghanistan.[20]

Apart from financial assistance, external backing is also thought to take the form of religious instruction and military training. The Philippine National Intelligence Coordinating Agency (NICA) maintains it has concrete proof that foreign nationals are currently residing in MILF camps, providing a variety of "educational" services ranging from theology classes to basic weapon-handling seminars.[21]

---

[18]Clamor, "Terrorism in the Philippines," p. 5; Filler, "Muslim Militancy," p. 16; and "Validation of the Existence of the ASG," unpublished paper prepared by the Philippine National Intelligence Coordinating Agency (NICA), February 14, 1997.

[19]Correspondence with PNP Directorate for Intelligence, Camp Crame, Manila, June 1998. See also "Held to Ransom," *Far Eastern Economic Review*, May 25, 2000; "Zambo Blast Coverup for Weak ASG," *The Manila Times* (Internet edition), January 5, 1999; and Filler, "Muslim Militancy," pp. 16–17.

[20]Correspondence with intelligence representatives from the PNP, NICA, and AFP, Manila, June 1998.

[21]Correspondence with the NICA, Quezon City, June 1998.

Moreover, Philippine authorities claim to have evidence that extremists and mercenaries from the Middle East and South Asia have traveled to Mindanao to train MILF cadres in the fundamentals of assassination, bombing, sabotage and, possibly, suicide attacks. [22]

MILF cadres are additionally alleged to have benefited from military training abroad, particularly in camps run ex-*Mujahideen* fighters located along the Pakistani-Afghan border. According to NICA officials, recruits travel to South Asia on the grounds that they are taking theological courses at the University of Pakistan. Once there, however, they are diverted to regional camps where they receive intensive instruction in unconventional warfare techniques.[23]   Of particular importance in this regard is a group known as *Al-Afghani*, a "freelance" organization that is alleged to have been providing external training for MILF (and Abu Sayyaf) cadres since at least 1994.[24]

The pertinence of international and regional linkages applies equally, if not more, to the Abu Sayyaf Group. Philippine military and police intelligence both assert that Abu Sayyaf members have benefited from overseas training, primarily in camps located in Pakistan and Afghanistan. As with the MILF, it is believed that the freelance *Al-Afghani* plays a critical role in this regard. Indeed, according to Philippine authorities, the Afghan influence is one of the strongest external influences currently being exerted on Abu Sayyaf. Officials with the Police Directorate for Intelligence believe this to be a legacy of the Abu Sayyaf leadership's intensive involvement in the Afghan war during the 1980s—a role which, at least in relative terms, was far more intimate than that of the MILF.[25]

---

[22]Correspondence with police and military intelligence, Manila, June 1998.

[23]It is also believed that a certain amount of MILF external training takes place in camps located in Sudan and Egypt, with MILF cadres, again, traveling overseas on the grounds that they are undertaking theological courses at foreign institutions. Correspondence with PNP Directorate for Intelligence, Manila, June 1998.

[24]Meetings with representatives from the AFP and PNP Directorate for Intelligence, Manila in September 1996 and June 1998. See also "March of the Militants," *Far Eastern Economic Review*, March 9, 1995; "Filipino Terrorists Using Pakistan as a 'Base of Operations,'" GMA-7 Radio Television Arts Network, Quezon City, April 16, 1995; and "Islamic Terrorism Tied to Pakistani University," *New York Times*, March 20, 1995.

[25]Correspondence with PNP Directorate for Intelligence, Camp Crame, Manila, June 1998.

In addition to overseas training, there is also evidence to suggest that Abu Sayyaf established formal operational and financial links with international terrorists and extremists. Philippine military intelligence believes that Abu Sayyaf, possibly in conjunction with renegade elements of the MILF, has facilitated local logistics for transnational Islamic organizations wishing to operate out of the Philippines, something that fits well with the group's international self-identity.[26] There is also concern that Abu Sayyaf has been instrumental in developing regional networks with radicals in Malaysia and Islamic rebels operating in Aceh and southern Thailand.[27] Fears of mutually supportive arms links have been further heightened in the wake of increased instability in Aceh, with regional threat assessments now focusing on the possibility of Cambodian arms shipments being trafficked to northern Sumatra, southern Thailand, and Mindanao.[28]

PROSPECTS FOR PEACE IN THE PHILIPPINES

Prospects for peace in Mindanao received a major boost in September 1996 when the MNLF signed the Davao Consensus, agreeing to end its campaign of armed violence and reintegrate into the mainstream of legitimate politics.[29] The accord provides for the

---

[26]See Peter Chalk, "Political Terrorism in Southeast Asia," Terrorism and Political Violence, Vol. 10, No. 2, 1998, pp. 126–28; Clamor, "Terrorism in the Philippines," p. 10; "The Shadow of Terrorism," Asiaweek, April 28, 1995; and "The Man Who Wasn't There," Time, February 20, 1995.

[27]Personal correspondence co-author Peter Chalk and Pinkerton's Risk Assessment Services (PRAS), November 1996.

[28]Correspondence with Dr. Alan Dupont, Australian National University, Canberra, November 1999. Similar comments were made during interviews with intelligence representatives from the Australian Office of National Assessments (ONA), Canberra, November 1999.

[29]Other than the Davao Consensus, there have been two other attempts to negotiate an end to the insurgency in Mindanao. The first was the Tripoli Agreement, which was signed in Libya in 1976 and provided for the creation of an autonomous enclave of all the (then) 13 provinces and nine cities of Mindanao, Sulu, and Palawan. The MNLF ultimately rejected the deal largely because Marcos failed to fully implement its autonomy provisions. The second was the Republic Act 6734, introduced into legislation by President Corazon Aquino in 1987. It aimed to fully implement the 1976 accord, but made the establishment of a Muslim enclave subject to referendum. Four provinces subsequently voted for inclusion (the same four provinces included in the

creation of an MNLF-led Council for Peace and Development to implement and coordinate peace and development projects throughout the 14 provinces in the southern Philippines as well as the creation of a separate, limited, four-district Muslim autonomous region. A referendum on the extension of this enclave is due in 2001.[30]

Although the Davao Consensus was instrumental in securing the endorsement of the MNLF, the MILF and Abu Sayyaf both categorically rejected the agreement. The MILF renounced the accord on the grounds that it failed to satisfy fundamental Muslim aspirations, particularly in regard to creating an independent Islamic state.[31] The uncompromising attitude of these two groups has been reflected in a southern Philippine region that continues to be wracked by incessant violence, with bombings, shootings, kidnappings, and, at times, full-scale military clashes.[32]

Given the present political context in the Philippines, any notion of granting independence to the south is out of the question. The existence of a Catholic majority (both within and outside Mindanao), which firmly upholds the vision of a fully unified and integrated Philippine Republic, ensures that no government would receive an electoral mandate to accede to the secessionist demands of a largely isolated Islamic minority. Most analysts concur that the best hope for effecting such an outcome lies with implementing a sustained economic development program. Achieving this would not only undermine the civilian support base of the insurgents, it would also

---

1996 agreement), an outcome that the MNLF rejected. For further details see Chalk, "The Davao Consensus," pp. 82–85.

[30]Chalk, "The Davao Consensus," pp. 85–86; Islam, "The Islamic Independence Movements in Patani of Thailand and Mindanao of the Philippines," p. 450.

[31]Correspondence with NICA, Manila, June 1998. See also Chalk, "The Davao Consensus," pp. 88–91; "The Moro Jihad," p. 12.

[32]James Clad notes that this incessant violence also reflects warlordism and gang competition as much as religiously targeted terrorist violence. It represents a type of continuity, Clad observes, with the practices of traditional leaders, from precolonial times, who routinely indulged in kidnapping, hostage-taking, slave-trading, and the like. Personal communication, January 2001.

remove both groups' *raison d'être*, necessarily forcing each to adopt a more pragmatic and conciliatory negotiating line with Manila.[33]

Little progress has been made in this direction, however, Mindanao's enormous economic potential notwithstanding.[34] Investment has also all but ground to a complete halt. The Manila government has been preoccupied with the fallout of the Asian economic malaise, which has undercut its own plans for macroeconomic reform and infrastructure development. And while foreign companies and corporations might be attracted by the southern Philippines' abundant supply of natural resources, the continuing lack of law and order in the region detracts from its reputation as a safe, long-term investment opportunity.[35]

MUSLIM SEPARATISM IN SOUTHERN THAILAND

Separatist violence in southern Thailand centers on the activities of the Malay Muslim population in the provinces of Pattani, Yala, and Narithiwat, which historically constituted part of the former Kingdom of Patani.[36] Three main pillars underscore Malay separatist

---

[33]Correspondence with Professor Aprodicio Laquian, University of British Columbia, Vancouver, July 1998. Professor Laquian refers to this as "the developmental strategy" for conflict resolution. See also "Held to Ransom," *Far Eastern Economic Review,* May 25, 2000. The example of the Paglas Corporation, a company that operates a US$35 million banana plantation in Maguindanao, can be offered in support of the "development strategy" thesis. According to the corporation's director, Ibrahim Pendatum Paglas, the plantation currently employs 2000 people, over half of whom are former MILF members.

[34]Mindanao has vast timber, agricultural, and mineral deposits at its disposal, not to mention substantial oil reserves.

[35]See "Philippines 'Achilles Heel' Threatens Its Economic Prosperity," *The Australian,* February 20, 1996; "Poor Little Dragon," *Foreign Report,* 2385, February 1996, pp. 5–6; "Campaign to Wipe Out Kidnappers in Philippines," *New Sunday Times,* March 13, 1997; "Southern Discomfort," *Far Eastern Economic Review,* February 19, 1998; and "When Travelers Are Targets: The Growing Threat of Kidnapping Abroad," *Washington Post,* July 12, 1998.

[36]This is the Malay spelling of Pattani. In Thai, the province is spelled with two "t"s. Muslims represent approximately 80 percent of the population in these three provinces. Malays also constitute a majority in the province of Satun, although in this case, Thai integrationist policies have been more successful, for two reasons: first, most people in Satun speak Thai in their everyday lives and, therefore, have not felt aggrieved by a sense of linguistic alienation. Second, the province's main links of

identity in this region. First is a belief in the traditional virtues and "greatness" of the Kingdom of Patani (*Patani Darussalam*). Second is identification with the Malay people, itself reinforced by repeated cross-border contacts with ethnic kin in the northern Malaysian province of Kelantan. Third is a religious orientation based on Islam.[37] These three ingredients are woven together in the principle of *hijra* (literally, "emigration in the 'cause of God'"), which asserts that all Islamic communities have both a religious right and duty to "withdraw" from any form of persecution that is serving to place their survival in jeopardy.[38] It is on the basis of this religious edict that Malay Muslim-instigated civil disobedience and separatist violence have been both justified and exonerated.

Ever since the Kingdom of Patani was brought under effective Siamese rule in the late 1700s, repeated attempts have been made to "Siam-ize" the local culture, language, and religion by enforcing uniformity in language and social behavior. Although such integrationist designs have not been directed solely at the Malay Muslims of southern Thailand, they have clearly constituted a direct threat to the region's particular ethno-religious identity.[39]

The underdeveloped nature of southern Thailand relative to the rest of the country merely compounded the sense of regional dissatisfaction, further fueling separatist designs and aspirations.[40] Two principal militant groups remain active in southern Thailand: PULO and New PULO. PULO is the largest and most prominent of the

---

communication are northward to Thailand, while road and rail access south to Malaysia is minimal.

[37]Connor Bailey and John Miksic, "The Country of Patani in the Period of Re-Awakening: A Chapter from Ibrahim Syukri's Sejarah Kerajaan Melayu Patani," in Andrew Forbes (ed.), *The Muslims of Thailand, Volume II: Politics of the Malay-Speaking South*, Centre for Southeast Asian Studies, Bihar, 1989, p. 151.

[38]Christie, *A Modern History of Southeast Asia*, p. 133.

[39]Ministry of Foreign Affairs, *Thai Muslims*, Bangkok, 1979, pp. 5–6; Muthiah Alagappa, *The National Security of Developing States: Lessons from Thailand*, (Acorn House, Massachusetts, 1987), pp. 204–07; R. J. May, "The Religious Factor in Three Minority Movements," *Contemporary Southeast Asia*, Vol. 13, No. 4, 1992, pp. 403–04.

[40]R. J. May, "The Religious Factor in Three Minority Movements," *Contemporary Southeast Asia*, Vol. 13, No. 4, 1992, p. 403; Christie, *A Modern History of Southeast Asia*, pp. 187–88; David Brown, *State and Ethnic Politics in Southeast Asia*, Routledge, London, 1994, pp. 166–70; and Michael Liefer, *Dictionary of the Modern Politics of Southeast Asia*, Routledge, London, 1996, p. 35.

various Malay Muslim groups that have operated in southern Thailand since the 1960s. The group sanctions violence as part of its secessionist struggle and recognizes the need to intensify international publicity on the plight of Pattani's Malay Muslims. Militant insurgent actions are carried out by a separate armed wing known as the Pattani United Liberation Army (PULA), which has claimed responsibility for several bomb and arson attacks against government establishments in the south.[41] Perceived symbols of Thai cultural dominance have also been periodically targeted, including schools and Buddhist temples.

The New PULO emerged as a dissident faction of PULO in 1995. The group has pursued the goal of Pattani self-autonomy through less dramatic but more consistent actions than its parent organization. To this end, the focus has been on minor attacks that are intended to repeatedly harass and pester police and local government authorities.[42] The choice of this particular *modus operandi* probably reflects a desire on the part of the New PULO leadership to conserve limited operational resources. It may also be indicative of an attempt to enhance the perceived legitimacy of the separatist Islamic struggle in the south by minimizing the scale of violence directed against people.

In general, PULO and New PULO have been largely unwilling to co-ordinate their operational activities, essentially because they have differences in strategic outlooks.[43] Nonetheless, the organizations did agree to form a tactical alliance in mid-1997 in an attempt to re-focus national and regional attention on the "southern question." Operating under the name of *Bersatu* (Solidarity), the two Pattani groups carried out a series of coordinated attacks (code-named "Falling Leaves") aimed at killing off state workers, law enforcement

---

[41]Peter Chalk, "Thailand," in Jason Isaacson and Colin Rubenstein (eds.), *Islam in Asia: Changing Political Realities*, (AJC and AIJAC, Washington, D.C., and Melbourne, 1999, p. 166.

[42]Correspondence with Thai Military Intelligence, Bangkok, July 1997. See also "Terrorist Suspect Has Violent Past," *The Sunday Nation*, January 25, 1998.

[43]Correspondence with Thai Military Intelligence, Bangkok, July 1997. See also Alagappa, *The National Security of Developing States*, 213; and "The Story Behind the Gerakan Mujahidin Islam Pattani," *The Bangkok Post*, January 18, 1998.

personnel, local government officials, schoolteachers and other perceived symbols of Thai repression.[44]

The external dimension of the PULO/New PULO separatist struggle
essentially relates to backing from Islamic militants in northern
Malaysia. Thailand has repeatedly alleged that the two groups have
benefited from the provision of safe haven in the State of Kelantan
and that support has come with the sanction of the province's ruling
Islamic Party (PAS) as well as the official indifference of the Kuala
Lumpur government. Somewhat more serious have been periodic
charges that radicals in Kelantan are facilitating the transshipment of
weapons from Cambodia to avail terrorist operations in southern
Thailand.[45]

The question of external Malaysian support assumed increased
prominence in late 1997 following the initiation of "Falling Leaves,"
an operation that Thai intelligence maintains could not have taken
place in the absence of PAS support. This assessment was
instrumental in heightening diplomatic tension between Bangkok
and Kuala Lumpur, with the Thai government specifically warning
that closer economic ties would be curtailed if cross-border
cooperation against PULO and New PULO was not considerably
stepped up.[46]

Concerned that this would jeopardize the much-touted Malaysia-
Indonesia-Thailand Growth Triangle (MITGT), Malaysian Prime
Minister Mahathir acceded to the Thai demands and personally
sanctioned joint police raids against secessionists thought to be
hiding in northern Malaysia. The resulting collaboration proved to
be a success, leading to the arrests of several PULO and New PULO

---

[44]Between August 1997 and January 1998, no fewer than 33 separate attacks were
carried out as part of this effort, resulting in nine deaths, several dozen injuries and
considerable economic damage. See Chalk, "Political Terrorism in Southeast Asia";
"Chronology of Southern Violence," *The Bangkok Post*, February 1, 1998.

[45]See, for instance, "Minister: 'Southern Separatists Receive Foreign Training,'" *The
Nation*, January 6, 1995; "Malaysia Denies Thai Terrorist Claims," *The Australian*,
January 6, 1998; and "Malaysia 'Not Training Ground for Thai Rebels,'" *The Straits
Times*, January 5, 1998; "Worse to Come," *Far Eastern Economic Review*, July 29, 1999.

[46]Correspondence with Tony Davis, Specialist correspondent with *Jane's Intelligence
Review*, Canberra, September 1998. See also "PM: Peace in South Vital to Growth
Triangle," *The Bangkok Post*, January 21, 1998.

leaders in early 1998. Strategically, this represented a major blow to both groups, encouraging many cadres to "give up the struggle." Indeed, in the months following the joint raids, over 900 militants from PULO, New PULO, and various other smaller groups voluntarily joined a government-sponsored "rehabilitation" program, pledging to become active participants in peaceful national development.[47] More significantly, several key leaders fled abroad.[48]

Notwithstanding these developments, it is still too early to conclude that armed separatism is at an end in southern Thailand. Malaysia always has the option to put pressure on Thailand by taking a less proactive role in blunting natural Malay sympathies for co-religionists in the southern Thai provinces. Although absolute growth rates are increasing, the region remains underdeveloped relative to other parts of Thailand, with an average per capita income of at least 7,000 baht less than in neighboring provinces. In addition, the south still exists against a backdrop of perceived linguistic and religious discrimination, and Muslim participation in local business is minimal. Both of these factors continue to feed at least residual feelings of discontent and frustration, hindering the prospects for true national reconciliation.[49]

---

[47]"50 Southern Separatists Surrender," *The Bangkok Post*, March 12, 1998; "Southern Rebels Surrender," and "Southern Rebels Meet Deadline to Surrender," *The Bangkok Post*, March 10, 1998.

[48]"Separatists in Malaysia Flee Abroad," *The Bangkok Post*, February 22, 1998; "Separatists Flee 'Haven,'" *The Bangkok Post*, February 26, 1998.

[49]Peter Chalk, *Grey Area Phenomena in Southeast Asia*, Strategic Defence Studies Centre, Canberra, Australia, 1997, p. 62; "Ties of Faith," *Far Eastern Economic Review*, April 11, 1996; and Ladd Thomas, "Thailand" in William Carpenter and David Wiencek (eds.), *Asian Security Handbook*, M. E. Sharpe, New York, 1996, pp. 242–43.

Chapter Ten

IMPLICATIONS FOR THE UNITED STATES AND THE U.S. AIR FORCE

The stakes for the United States in Indonesia are enormous. The outcome of Indonesia's democratic experiment will have a major impact in shaping the security environment in Asia. If Indonesia's transition to democracy is successful, Indonesia will be the world's third largest democracy as well as the largest democracy in the Muslim world. A stable, strong, and democratic Indonesia could resume its leadership role in ASEAN, further regional integration on democratic principles, contribute to maintaining stability in Southeast Asia, and deter potential Chinese adventurism.

On the other hand, democracy in Indonesia may not necessarily foster stability. An unstable democracy could decay into increased political chaos and ethnic and religious strife or lead to overt or disguised military rule. Under these circumstances, a return to a more authoritarian form of government but with better governance, legitimization through elections, and the prospect of future democratic evolution may be the most practical formula for restoring stability and regional security.

An unstable or disintegrating Indonesia would make the regional security environment unpredictable, create opportunities for forces seeking to subvert the regional status quo, and generate greater demands on the United States and the U.S. military. Indonesia's geopolitical weight makes it the bedrock of Southeast Asia. If Indonesia were to disintegrate or become "Burmanized," that is, regress into a repressive pariah state, the loss, not only to the Indonesian people but also to the cause of democracy and stability in Asia, would be enormous. Without a cohesive Indonesia, Southeast

Asia will be weak at its core, making it easier for China to extend its influence and complicating U.S. efforts to maintain the regional balance of power.

The first priority is to support Indonesia's stability and territorial integrity.

This would appear obvious, but the mix of policies that emerges from the U.S. policy process—reflecting the priorities of competing bureaucracies and foreign policy constituencies—are not always well designed to advance core U.S. security interests. An effective U.S. approach should focus on fundamentals. First, the United States should work with Japan, other regional allies, and international financial institutions to provide the resources needed to assist Indonesia in overcoming its multiple crises. Second, support for Indonesia's democratization and stability should not be made contingent on the resolution of second-tier issues. Third, the United States and the international community should refrain from demanding more than the weakened Indonesian government can deliver at this time, particularly on issues that touch on sensitive sovereignty concerns. In this regard, it is important to be cognizant of how giving or withholding aid for Indonesia plays in Indonesian politics—a miscue could result in weakening rather than strengthening Indonesian democratic forces. It is also important to get the *tone* of the United States' public dialogue with Indonesia right. As former Australian Foreign Minister Gareth Evans noted, there is a powerful instinct in Indonesia to oppose foreign pressure and to react sharply to condescending foreign advice.[1]

The second priority is to engage the Indonesian military.

The military will play a critical role in Indonesia's evolution. The United States has an opportunity to influence the thinking of the Indonesian military at a time when the military is looking for a new model and is open to new ideas. Military-to-military ties were suspended in September 1999 because of the Indonesian military's role in the violence in East Timor in the wake of the independence referendum. Following Under Secretary of State Thomas Pickering's

---

[1]Presentation at U.S.-Indonesia Society (USINDO), Open Forum, Washington, D.C., December 12, 2000.

visit to Jakarta in March 2000, the U.S. government began to take some steps to resume military cooperation.   There was a limited resumption of Indonesian participation in combined exercises. Some ten Indonesian air force officers (but none from the army) participated in the annual Cobra Gold exercise in Thailand, at the invitation of the Thai air force.[2] Exercises were scheduled with Indonesian marines concentrating on humanitarian assistance and disaster relief.[3] Even this limited progress was reversed by the killing of three UN workers in West Timor in September 2000 (see Chapter Three).

The loss of International Military Education and Training (IMET) funding for Indonesia has had a significant impact on Indonesian military attitudes toward the United States. Halted initially in 1992 after the shooting of civilians in East Timor, some limited funds were restored through the Expanded IMET Program in 1993, but cut again in 1999. The Indonesian military has been isolated from U.S. military education programs ever since. The lack of exposure to U.S. values and the attenuation of personal ties between U.S. and Indonesian officers may well be a contributing factor to the rising tide of anti-American sentiment among senior and mid-level Indonesian military officers today.[4]

Engagement with the Indonesian military would improve the ability of the United States to promote a democratic model of military professionalism in Indonesia and to play a role in fostering intra-ASEAN defense cooperation and interoperability.

The United States should also provide assistance to prevent the further deterioration of Indonesian defense capabilities. The escalating violence in parts of Indonesia makes rapid deployment of troops to trouble spots a critical need, but the suspension of U.S. military assistance to Indonesia—particularly the restrictions on the transfer of military equipment and spare parts—has affected the ability of the

---

[2]Haseman, presentation at USINDO Conference.

[3]"United States and Indonesia quietly resume military cooperation," *New York Times,* May 24, 2000.

[4]Contribution by Colonel John B. Haseman, U.S. Army (ret.), November 7, 2000.

armed forces to transport troops to areas of violence on a timely basis.

As a first step, the deepening of the military-to-military relationship could begin with the Indonesian air force and the navy. Unlike the army, the air force and the navy by and large were not involved in internal security operations and the human rights abuses that have been reported in that context. Moreover, they are in greater need of military equipment, spare parts, and technical assistance to perform their defense functions. As an Indonesian air force general observed, Indonesia is an archipelago of 17,000 islands that can be linked only by air. However, the air force has been hurt by the U.S. restrictions on military equipment sales. With only half of their C-130s operational, it takes the military 10 to 15 days to transport men and equipment by ground in some parts of Indonesia. Rebuilding Indonesia's air transport capability should be a priority in the U.S.-Indonesian defense relationship.

The third priority is to help rebuild a constructive Indonesian role in regional security.

This would be necessarily a long-term goal, because Indonesia is unlikely to resume its leadership role in Southeast Asia until the country overcomes its current domestic difficulties. The United States could move the process forward by helping to restore the Indonesian-Australian security relationship, which was in the past an important element of the Southeast Asian security architecture. The Australian-Indonesian relationship is driven, of course, by its own dynamics, which took a turn for the worse as the result of the East Timor crisis. Indonesians, both civilian and military, resented Australia's role in the East Timor crisis and perceived pretension to regional primacy. At the same time, in discussions in Jakarta with senior Indonesian military officers in March 2000 some Indonesian interlocutors acknowledged that Indonesia and Australia have interests in common and that cooperation would enhance the Republic's security.[5] The United States, as a treaty ally of Australia and friend of

---

[5]A senior Indonesian air force officer said that the Australian and Indonesian air forces were cooperating in surveillance of the Timor Gap—a task that the Indonesians do not have the capabilities to do by themselves.

Indonesia, can play an important role in facilitating a rapprochement between these two key regional actors.

A key part of the rebuilding of a constructive Indonesian role in regional security is a permanent solution in East Timor, which equates to a stable, independent East Timor and a constructive relationship between Indonesia and East Timor. Attaining this goal will require a two-pronged strategy:

First, promoting the negotiation of an arrangement that takes into account the interests of all sides. Such a settlement would make possible the return of refugees and the closing of the camps in West Timor and should include the cessation of all Indonesian support for recalcitrant militia elements.

Second, organizing an international effort to train and equip an East Timorese security force capable of securing the border and protecting the East Timorese population.

Over the longer term, if Indonesia is successful in completing its transition to a stable democracy, the United States and Indonesia should develop a closer defense relationship, comparable to the relationship the United States has with other friends and allies in the region. A cooperative security relationship with Indonesia may also involve arrangements for U.S. access and basing. As noted in previous RAND studies on Asian security, a portfolio approach to U.S. basing rights would help to reduce the risk that internal instabilities and weak governments could threaten loss of, or timely and unhindered access to, military facilities in the region. Access to bases in Indonesia would also compensate for the space limitations that constrain U.S. aircraft currently deployed on a rotational basis to Singapore. Such access could be particularly valuable in the event of a sharp deterioration in the regional security environment.

The fourth priority is to support the development of a regional crisis reaction force.

Over the past several years, ASEAN countries have developed a network of informal bilateral defense ties, manifested in mutual use of military facilities, expanded military contacts, and joint defense exercises. Singapore's proposal for a regional armed force to respond to crises, if accepted by other ASEAN states, could be an important step in strengthening ASEAN's security role. The United States could contribute to this evolution by promoting inter-operability with and among friendly ASEAN states and, if needed, providing support capabilities for the effective deployment and operation of an ASEAN military force in a crisis.

BIBLIOGRAPHY

BOOKS

Alagappa, Muthiah, *The National Security of Developing States: Lessons from Thailand*, Acorn House, Massachusetts, 1987.

Baker, Richard W., et al. (eds.), *Indonesia: the Challenge of Change*, Institute of Southeast Asian Studies (ISEAS), Singapore; St. Martin's Press, New York, 1999.

Bresnan, John, *Managing Indonesia*, Columbia University Press, New York, 1993.

Brown, David, *State and Ethnic Politics in Southeast Asia*, Routledge, London, 1994.

Catley, Bob, and Makmur Keliat, *Spratlys: The Dispute in the South China Sea*, Ashgate, Aldershot, United Kingdom, 1997.

Chalk, Peter, *Grey Area Phenomena in Southeast Asia*, Strategic Defence Studies Centre, Canberra, Australia, 1997.

Chalk, Peter, "Political Terrorism in Southeast Asia," *Terrorism and Political Violence*, Vol. 10, No. 2, 1998.

Christie, Clive J., *A Modern History of Southeast Asia*, I. B. Tauris, London, 1996.

Cotton, James (ed.), *East Timor and Australia*, Australian Defence Studies Centre, Canberra, 1999.

Cribb, Robert, and Colin Brown, *Modern Indonesia: A History Since 1945*, Longman, London and New York, 1995.

Fox, James J., and Dionisio Babo Soares (eds.), *Out of the Ashes: The Destruction and Reconstruction of East Timor*, Crawford Press, Adelaide, Australia, 2000.

George, T. J., *Revolt in Mindanao: The Rise of Islam in Philippine Politics*, Oxford University Press, New York, 1980.

Han Sung-Joo, *Changing Values in Asia: Their Impact on Governance and Development*, Japan Center for International Exchange and Institute of Southeast Asian Studies (ISEAS), Singapore, 1999.

Heidhues, Mary F. Sommers, *Southeast Asia's Chinese Minorities*, Longman, Australia, 1974.

Indorf, Hans, *Impediments to Regionalism in Southeast Asia*, Institute for Southeast Asian Studies (ISEAS), Singapore, 1984.

International Institute for Strategic Studies, *The Military Balance 1998/99*, Oxford University Press.

Isaacson, Jason, and Colin Rubenstein (eds.), *Islam in Asia: Changing Political Realities*, American Jewish Committee and Australia-Israel Jewish Affairs Committee, Washington, D.C., and Melbourne, 1999.

Knowles, James, Ernesto Pernia, and Mary Racelis, *Social Consequences of the Financial Crisis in Asia*, Asian Development Bank, Manila, July 1999.

Liddle, R. William, *Leadership and Culture in Indonesian Politics*, Allen and Unwin, Sydney, 1996.

Liefer, Michael, *Dictionary of the Modern Politics of Southeast Asia*, Routledge, London, 1996.

Lim Joo Jock and S. Vani (eds.), *Armed Separatism in Southeast Asia*, Institute of Southeast Asian Studies (ISEAS), Singapore, 1984.

Lim Joo Jock and S. Vani (eds.), *Armed Separatism in Southern Thailand*, Institute for Southeast Asian Studies (ISEAS), Singapore, 1984.

Lombard, Denys, *Le Sultanat d'Atjeh au Temps d'Iskandar Muslim 1607–1636*, Ecole Francaise d'Extreme-Orient, Paris, 1967.

May, R. J., "The Wild West in the South: A Recent Political History," in Mark Turner, R. J. May, and Lulu Respall Turner (eds.), *Mindanao: Land of Unfulfilled Promise*, New Day Publishers, Quezon City, Philippines, 1992.

Morrison, Charles E. (ed.), *Asia Pacific Security Outlook 1999*, ASEAN Institute for Strategic and International Studies, East-West Center, and Japan Center for International Exchange, Tokyo and New York, 1999.

Noer, John H., *Chokepoints: Maritime Economic Concerns in Southeast Asia*, National Defense University, Washington, D.C., 1996.

Schwarz, Adam, *A Nation in Waiting: Indonesia in the 1990s*, Westview, Boulder, 1994.

Soedjati Djiwandono and Yong Mun Cheong (eds.), *Soldiers and Stability in Southeast Asia*, Institute of Southeast Asian Studies (ISEAS), Singapore, 1988.

Sokolsky, Richard, Angel Rabasa, and C. R. Neu, *The Role of Southeast Asia in U.S. Strategy Toward China*, RAND, MR-1170-AF, 2000.

Tarling, Nicholas, *Nations and States in Southeast Asia*, Cambridge University Press, New York, 1998.

Thomas, Ladd, "Thailand," in William Carpenter and David Wiencek (eds.), *Asian Security Handbook*, M. E. Sharpe, New York, 1996.

Turner, Mark, R. J. May, and Lulu Respall Turner (eds.), *Mindanao: Land of Unfulfilled Promise*, New Day Publishers, Quezon City, Philippines, 1992.

U.S. Department of Commerce, *Statistical Abstract of the United States*, 1998.

Vatikiotis, Michael, *Indonesian Politics Under Suharto: Order and Pressure for Change*, Routledge, London, 1993.

Warshaw, Steven, *Southeast Asia Emerges*, Diablo Press, Berkeley, California, 1987.

Woodward, Mark R. (ed.), *Toward a New Paradigm: Recent Developments in Indonesian Islamic Thought*, Arizona State University Press, Tucson, 1996.

Wurfel, David, and Bruce Burton (eds.), *Southeast Asia in the New World Order*, St. Martin's Press, New York, 1996.

Zartman, I. William (ed.), *Collapsed States: the Disintegration and Restoration of Legitimate Authority*, Lynne Rienner Publishers, Boulder and London, 1995.

MONOGRAPHS, ARTICLES, AND PAPERS

Alhadar, Smith, "The Forgotten War in North Maluku," *Inside Indonesia*, No. 63, July-September 2000.

Almonte, Jose T., "Decentralization in the Philippines: Prospects, Impediments, and Challenges," paper presented at the CSCAP Seminar on Indonesia's Future Challenges and Implications for the Region," Jakarta, March 8, 2000.

Bjornlund, Eric, "Supporting the Democratic Transition Process in Indonesia," statement before the U.S. House of Representatives, Committee on International Relations, Subcommittee on Asia and the Pacific, February 16, 2000.

Centre for Strategic Studies, Victoria University of Wellington, New Zealand, "Strategic and Military Lessons from East Timor," CSS Strategic Briefing Papers, Vol. 2, Part 1, February 2000.

Chalk, Peter, "The Davao Consensus: A Panacea for the Muslim Insurgency in Mindanao?" *Terrorism and Political Violence*, Vol. 9, No. 2, 1997.

Chalk, Peter, "Contemporary Maritime Piracy in Southeast Asia," *Studies in Conflict and Terrorism*, Vol. 21, No. 1, 1998.

Chalk, Peter, "Maritime Piracy: A Global Overview," *Jane's Intelligence Review*, Vol. 12, No. 8, 2000.

Chalk, Peter, "Political Terrorism in Southeast Asia," *Terrorism and Political Violence*, Vol. 10, No. 2, 1998.

Clad, James, "Fin de Siecle, Fin de l'ASEAN?" Pacific Forum CSIS, *PacNet Newsletter,* March 3, 2000.

Clad, James, "Security in Southeast Asia," in William M. Carpenter and David G. Wiencek (eds.), *Asian Security Handbook 2000,* M. E. Sharpe, New York and London, 2000.

Clamor, Concepcion, "Terrorism in the Philippines and Its Impact on National and Regional Security," paper delivered before the CSCAP Working Group on Transnational Crime, Manila, May 1998.

Cloughley, Brian, "Indonesia fights domestic diversity," *Jane's International Defense Review,* September 1997.

Costello, Michael A., "The demography of Mindanao," in Mark Turner, R. J. May, and Lulu Respall Turner (eds.), *Mindanao: Land of Unfulfilled Promise,* New Day Publishers, Quezon City, Philippines, 1992.

Crouch, Harold, "The TNI and East Timor Policy," in James J. Fox and Dionisio Babo Soares (eds.), *Out of the Ashes: The Destruction and Reconstruction of East Timor,* Crawford Press, Adelaide, 2000.

Davis, Anthony, "Islamic Guerrillas Threaten Fragile Peace on Mindanao," *Jane's Intelligence Review,* Vol. 10, No. 5, May 1998.

Dynamic Research and Media Services, "A Study of the New Developments on the MNLF Secession Movement in Relation to AFP Plans," Office of the Deputy Chief of Staff for Plans, Quezon City, Philippines, 1989.

Emmerson, Donald, "Indonesia in Crisis: the Eerie Autonomy of Politics," Asian Security Policy Breakfast, Washington, D.C., October 1, 1998.

Emmerson, Donald, "Indonesia's Eleventh Hour in Aceh," *PacNet* 49, December 17, 1999.

Erawan, Ketut Putra, "Political Reform and Regional Politics in Indonesia," *Asian Survey,* Vol. 39, No. 4, 1999.

Federation of American Scientists, "Intelligence Resource Program: Free Aceh Movement," http://www.fas.org/irp/world/para/aceh.htm.

FitzSimons, Nina, "West Papua in 1999," *Inside Indonesia*, No. 61, January-March 2000.

Forbes, Andrew (ed.), *The Muslims of Thailand, Volume II: Politics of the Malay-Speaking South*, Centre for Southeast Asian Studies, Bihar, India, 1989.

Friend, Theodore, "Indonesia: Confronting the Political and Economic Crisis," testimony before the U.S. House of Representatives, Committee on International Relations, Subcommittee on Asia and the Pacific, February 16, 2000.

Habib, A. Hasnan, "The Future of the Indonesian Armed Forces," paper presented at the CSCAP Seminar on Indonesia's Future Challenges and Implications for the Region, Jakarta, March 8, 2000.

Haseman, John B., "The Misuse of Military Power and Misplaced Military Pride," in James J. Fox and Dionisio Babo Soares (eds.), *Out of the Ashes: The Destruction and Reconstruction of East Timor*, Crawford Press, Adelaide, 2000.

Human Rights Watch, "Why Aceh is Exploding," http://www.igc.org/hrw/campaigns/indonesia/aceh0827.htm.

International Crisis Group, *Indonesia's Crisis: Chronic But Not Acute*, ICG Indonesia Report No. 2, Jakarta/Brussels, May 31, 2000.

International Crisis Group, *Indonesia: Keeping the Military Under Control*, ICG Asia Report No. 9, Jakarta/Brussels, September 5, 2000.

International Monetary Fund, *IMF Concludes Article IV Consultation with Indonesia*, Public Information Notice No. 99/33, April 13, 1999.

International Monetary Fund, Memorandum of Economic and Financial Policies, Government of Indonesia and Bank Indonesia, http://www.imf.org/external/NP/LOI/idn/03/.

Islam, Syed Serajul, "The Islamic Independence Movements in Patani of Thailand and Mindanao of the Philippines," *Asian Survey*, Vol. 38, No. 5, May 1998.

Johanson, Vanessa, "The Sultan Will Be Dr. Hasan Tiro," *Inside Indonesia*, No. 60, 1999, gopher://gopher.igc.apc.org:2998/OREG-INDONESIA/r.945369609.23764.55.

Kingsbury, Damien, "The Reform of the Indonesian Armed Forces," *Contemporary Southeast Asia*, Vol. 22, No. 2, August 2000.

Lucero, Daniel, "The SPCPD: A Breakthrough Towards Peace," *Office of Strategic Studies (OSS) Digest*, July-August 1996.

May, R. J., "The Religious Factor in Three Minority Movements," *Contemporary Southeast Asia*, Vol. 13, No. 4, 1992.

Misra, A., "Guerrillas in the Mist," *Pioneer*, July 11, 1994.

Nalapat, M. D., "Historic chance for RI's military," *Jakarta Post*, March 3, 2000.

Roth, Stanley, "Indonesia: Confronting the Political and Economic Crisis," testimony before the U.S. House of Representatives, Committee on International Relations, Subcommittee on Asia and the Pacific, February 16, 2000.

Severino, Rodolfo C., "Indonesia and the Future of ASEAN," paper presented at the CSCAP Seminar on Indonesia's Future Challenges and Implications for the Region," Jakarta, March 9, 2000.

Shiraishi, Takashi, "The Indonesian Military in Politics" unpublished paper, 1998.

Sinha, P. B., "Muslim Insurgency in the Philippines," *Strategic Analysis*, Vol. 18, No. 5, 1995.

Smith, Anthony L., "Indonesia's Foreign Policy Under Abdurrahman Wahid: Radical or Status Quo State?" *Contemporary Southeast Asia*, Vol. 22, No. 3, December 2000.

Smith, Anthony L., "Indonesia's Role in ASEAN: The End of Leadership?" *Contemporary Southeast Asia*, Vol. 21, No. 2, August 1999

Smith, James P., Duncan Thomas, Elizabeth Frankenberg, Kathleen Beegle, and G. Teruel, "Wages, employment, and economic shocks: Evidence from Indonesia," Labor and Population Program, Working Papers Series 00-07, DRU-2319-1-NICHD, RAND, October 2000.

Soesastro, Hadi, "Implications of Indonesia's Crisis for the Asia Pacific Region: A Literature Survey," May 8, 2000, http://www.pacific.net.id/hadisusastro/000508.html

Tan Sri Zainal Abidin Sulong, "The Regional Impact and the Role of the Region in Indonesia's Transformation," paper presented at the CSCAP Seminar on Indonesia's Future Challenges and Implications for the Region," Jakarta, March 9, 2000.

Tiwon, Sylvia, "From heroes to rebels," *Inside Indonesia*, No. 62, April-June 1999.

Tjokropranolo, *General Sudirman: the leader who finally destroyed Colonialism in Indonesia*, Australian Defence Studies Centre, Canberra, 1995.

Turner, Mark, "Terrorism and Secession in the Southern Philippines: The Rise of the Abu Sayyaf," *Contemporary Southeast Asia*, Vol. 17, No. 1, 1995.

U.S. Committee for Refugees, "The Political History of Aceh," http://www.refugees.org/news/crisis/indonesia/aceh.htm.

U.S. Department of Defense, "The United States Strategy for the East Asia-Pacific Region," Internet, 1998.

Van Langenberg, Michael, "End of the Jakartan Empire?" *Inside Indonesia*, No. 61, January-March 2000.

Wolfowitz, Paul, "A Muslim leader with a difference," *Wall Street Journal*, November 11, 1999.

Young, Thomas-Durell, "Australian Security and Defense Posture: Implications for Effecting Greater Cooperation," discussion paper, Pentagon Study Group on Japan and Northeast Asia, July 24, 2000.

NEWSPAPERS AND PERIODICALS

Asian Survey

Asian Wall Street Journal

Asiaweek

The Australian

The Bangkok Post

The Bulletin of Indonesian Economic Studies

Contemporary Southeast Asia (ISEAS Singapore)

The Economist

Far Eastern Economic Review

The Guardian (United Kingdom)

The Indonesian Observer (Jakarta)

The Indonesian Quarterly (Jakarta)

Inside Indonesia

Jane's Defence Weekly

Jakarta Post

Kompas (Jakarta)

Kyrway Report (Jakarta)

The Nation

New York Times

PacNet Newsletter, Center for Strategic and International Studies (CSIS), Washington, D.C.

The Philippine Daily Inquirer

The Straits Times (Singapore)

The Sydney Morning Herald

Wall Street Journal

Weekly Update, International Republic Institute, Washington, D.C.

West Papua Action Update (http://westpapuaaction.buz.org/latest-news.htm)

CONFERENCES

Conference for Security Cooperation in the Asia Pacific (CSCAP) International Seminar on Indonesia's Future Challenges and Implications for the Region, Jakarta, March 8, 2000.

Paul H. Nitze School of Advanced International Studies (SAIS) Seminar on East Timor, Washington, D.C., September 22, 1999.

Paul H. Nitze School of Advanced International Studies (SAIS) and Japan External Trade Organization Seminar (JETRO), Conference on Business Prospects in Indonesia Under the New Government, Washington, D.C., December 7, 1999.

United States-Indonesia Society (USINDO), "Parliamentary Elections in Indonesia: Consensus, Coalitions, or Confusion?" *Proceedings of USINDO Workshop*, Washington, D.C., June 22, 1999.

United States-Indonesia Society (USINDO), Conference on East Timor, Washington, D.C., September 10, 1999.

United States-Indonesia Society (USINDO), "Indonesia's Military: Backbone of the Nation or Achilles' Heel?" *Proceedings of USINDO Workshop*, Washington, D.C., March 28, 2000.

United States-Indonesia Society (USINDO), Open Forum with Dr. Paul Michael Taylor, "Turbulent Times Past and Present in the Moluccas," Washington, D.C., September 13, 2000.

United States-Indonesia Society (USINDO), Open Forum with Dr. Rizal Ramli, Coordinating Minister for Economic Affairs, Washington, D.C., September 26, 2000.

United States-Indonesia Society (USINDO), Open Forum with Dr. Amien Rais, Chairman of the People's Consultative Assembly, Washington, D.C., October 30, 2000.

United States-Indonesia Society (USINDO), Open Forum with Dr. Jusuf Wanandi, Chairman, Jakarta Center for Strategic and International Studies, Washington, D.C., December 5, 2000.